HAVING VICTORY OVER SELF- SABOTAGING BEHAVIOUR

FINDING HOPE THROUGH FAITH AND PSYCHOLOGY

D. R. YOUNG

Published by Hemingway Publishers

Cover design by Hemingway Publishers

ISBN: Printed in the United States

Table of Contents

Introduction

Have you ever wondered why, despite your best intentions, success and happiness seem just out of reach? Maybe it's that Monday morning push, one more snooze button, even when you promised yourself last night would mark a new beginning. Or perhaps it's the way you brush off a genuine compliment at work with self-deprecating humor, as if admitting your worth is somehow taboo. Have you ever walked away from an important conversation, replaying every word and wishing you'd spoken up for yourself, but deep down knowing you held back because you were afraid of rocking the boat, or maybe, afraid of what thriving might really look like? If any of this sounds familiar, you're not alone. In fact, you're in good company.

Almost all of us have moments where we trip ourselves up without even realizing it, quietly undermining our deepest hopes and goals. Sometimes it's as subtle as procrastinating a task that matters to our future or doubting our talents right when we need them most. Other times, it's bigger, self-destructive patterns that repeat in our careers, relationships, or spiritual life, always leaving us wondering why change feels impossible. Sometimes we tell ourselves, "That's just who I am," or we chalk it up to bad luck or other people's actions. But what if, beneath all those explanations, there's something deeper at play? What if the biggest roadblock is not external, but inside us?

This book is about shining a light on that hidden enemy, self-sabotage, and showing you that you are not powerless against it. Self-sabotage is tricky; it wears many disguises: perfectionism, chronic indecision, numbing behaviors, sabotage of relationships, anxiety spirals, and the slow erosion of self-worth. Most importantly, it doesn't mean you're lazy, broken, or a failure. It means you're human. But you don't have to stay stuck.

Here's the truth nobody likes to say out loud: recognizing the ways we get in our own way can feel shameful. Admitting our flaws isn't celebrated in most cultures; it's often treated as proof of weakness or lack of discipline. We're taught to strive, hustle, fix ourselves, and project confidence. So when cycles of self-defeat show up again and again, we hide behind busyness, humor, or distraction rather than face them head-on. And yet, freedom begins exactly where honesty meets compassion. True transformation doesn't start with self-condemnation, but with understanding.

My goal in these pages is not to condemn, scold, or shame you. I've wrestled with self-sabotage in my own story, wrestled and, eventually, found a way through. As someone who has researched the psychology of behavior and journeyed through Christian faith, I'm passionate about unraveling the knots between our thoughts, feelings, choices, and spiritual battles. Over the years, I've helped individuals uncover the roots of their destructive cycles and rediscover hope, purpose, and lasting change. I want to share with you what actually works, what I've learned through evidence-based practice, personal mess, and timeless biblical wisdom.

You'll gain more here than awareness. Yes, you'll finally see those old patterns for what they are, not unsolvable mysteries, but habits with causes and solutions. We'll dig into how early experiences, beliefs, and cultural messages secretly program us to get in our own way. At the same time, you'll find out how spiritual truths offer real-life strategies for breaking free. By the end of our journey together, you will be empowered: to change resistant patterns, restore broken relationships, heal anxious or depressed minds, and walk boldly into the life you were designed for.

Let's be honest: facing self-sabotage may feel daunting or even embarrassing at first. You might worry that looking at your shortcomings equals admitting defeat. Culture tends to glorify instant success and relentless positivity; struggling is swept under the rug, especially in church circles where faith sometimes gets confused with flawless living. But here's the good news: every single person reading this struggles at some level with getting in their own way. It's part of the human condition. The only difference is whether we choose to confront it or keep pretending it's not there.

If you recognize yourself in these pages, I want you to know you're seen. You won't find any lectures here, just compassionate truth, practical tools, and hope rooted in grace. Whether your patterns show up in your family life, career, friendships, or quiet moments of self-talk, it's possible to break the cycle. And the path forward is both scientific and spiritual: understanding the mind God gave you, learning to rewire it, and anchoring your identity in Christ rather than old limitations.

What does this journey look like? First, we'll tackle the basics: what is self-sabotage, and how does it sneak into everyday life? Together, we'll learn to name its forms, from subtle self-doubt to outright derailing our best opportunities. Next, we'll examine real-life examples from both the Bible and today's world, recognizing how even heroes struggled with self-defeating choices (and what we can learn from their victories and failures alike).

Then we move deeper, exploring the costs, how self-sabotage damages our most important relationships, and chips away at mental well-being. We'll look at how anxiety and depression often spring from unhealed wounds and warped self-perceptions, and how these emotional storms feed right back into destructive cycles. But we won't stop with diagnosis; we'll press on to healing, covering specific, research-backed strategies and faith-based practices that create real and lasting change, not just short-term motivation.

Practical exercises will help you dismantle negative habits and replace them with "victory habits," tools for strengthening resilience, building meaningful connections, and experiencing true joy. We'll also address the big questions of identity:

Who are you, truly, apart from your mistakes or doubts?

How do you step into your God-given potential, not just by trying harder, but by seeing yourself differently, through the eyes of grace?

Finally, we'll paint a picture of what sustainable freedom looks like, not perfection, but ongoing growth rooted in healthy patterns, restored thinking, and a vibrant relationship with Christ.

Throughout this book, you'll notice something unique: every chapter integrates psychological insight with spiritual truth. You won't be asked to choose between science and faith; instead, you'll discover how the two work hand in hand, uncovering both the emotional and the spiritual roots of sabotage, and offering a roadmap toward wholeness. My promise to you is that you'll finish these chapters not just with knowledge, but with a renewed sense of possibility, a conviction that you really can leave old patterns behind and step forward with purpose.

If you're tired of watching dreams slip away for reasons you can't explain, if you're done dismissing your strengths or living less than you're called to, this book is for you. If you long for healthier relationships, restored confidence, and peace where anxiety once ruled, come along. The struggle with self-sabotage is real, but so is the hope for freedom.

Are you ready to see yourself honestly, love yourself generously, and live from the power that God meant for you?

If so, let's begin.

The breakthrough you've been waiting for starts here.

Chapter One
Unveiling the Enemy Within

Did you know that many adults unknowingly stand in their own way, making choices that hold them back from success and happiness? It's surprising how common it is to act against our best interests without even realizing it. These hidden habits can feel like second nature, blending into everyday life so seamlessly that we barely notice the damage they cause. Why do we hesitate when opportunity knocks? What keeps us stuck in patterns that limit our growth? You are invited to uncover these quiet struggles and are offered fresh insights into the forces that shape our actions and the reasons it's so hard to break free.

Self-sabotage can show up in daily life wearing many different masks, often creeping in as habits or patterns that seem ordinary on the surface. For most adults, the idea that they are acting against their own happiness feels surprising, perhaps even impossible. Yet, self-sabotaging behaviors often serve as invisible barriers, quietly shaping choices and rerouting progress without anyone really noticing. These behaviors are rarely intentional; they often begin as coping strategies designed to protect against discomfort, pain, or disappointment. But over time, they might become so natural that they feel like a part of who we are.

Procrastination, a word I didn't know until college days, is one of the easiest places to spot self-sabotage, although it rarely feels that way. Imagine a parent who waits until the last minute to complete a work presentation, telling themselves they "work better under pressure." Beneath the surface, this delay might not be about laziness or poor time management. Instead, it could be an unconscious attempt to avoid the anxiety that comes with the risk of underperforming or being judged. By leaving little time, the person gives themselves an excuse if things do not go well: "I didn't fail, I just didn't have enough time." This habit protects their self-esteem but also prevents them from experiencing the satisfaction of doing their best.

Perfectionism, something that many struggle with, is another shape that self-sabotage can take. To the outside world, a perfectionist might seem thorough, dedicated, and highly motivated. Inside, there can be a lurking fear of criticism. By constantly tweaking, editing, and revising, the perfectionist delays sharing their work, avoiding the possibility of rejection. Take, for example, someone who writes and rewrites a cover letter for weeks, never quite feeling it is ready to submit for a dream job. The pursuit of perfection keeps them busy but ultimately holds them back from seizing new opportunities. In this way, the quest for high standards becomes a clever disguise for resistance.

Avoidance, often connected to attachments, is another familiar costume for self-sabotage. Emotional discomfort, uncertainty, or potential disappointment are all things the mind tries to sidestep. Someone may repeatedly decline invitations to social gatherings, not because they dislike people, but because they are afraid of awkwardness or rejection. This avoidance can provide short-term relief, making life feel safer. However, in the long term, it limits opportunities for connection, growth, and happiness, often leading to unnecessary loneliness.

Consider Clara, who dreams of moving to a new city for better work and a fresh start. Each time she plans to research apartments or update her resume, she tells herself she is too tired, too busy, or that there's always next week. Her days fill with urgent but unimportant chores. On a conscious level, she wants change, but deep down, she is protecting herself from the unknown, maybe the unresolved pain of rejection. The comfort of routine, even if unstimulating, feels less risky than the prospect of change. For Clara, these small acts of postponement and distraction add up to a pattern that keeps her life standing still.

These habits are not accidental. They are often learned responses from earlier experiences, where sidestepping pain or disappointment brought relief. Over time, procrastination, perfectionism, and avoidance become familiar solutions, so much so that most people rarely question them. The mind learns that avoiding discomfort, whether that's fear of failure, embarrassment, or rejection, means safety. Psychologists refer to this as avoidance learning. Each time a person sidesteps a stressful situation, the mind records that as a success, even if the action quietly steals away future chances for joy or accomplishment.

Often, adults continue these patterns even after the threat of old wounds has passed. For instance, growing up with high expectations may train someone to fear making mistakes, believing even small errors could lead to criticism. Habits rooted in childhood, like hesitating to speak up, putting aside personal desires, or giving up before starting, can survive well into adulthood, even when those fears no longer fit the current reality. Self-sabotage persists because it offers comfort and familiarity. These actions can feel like a shield, protecting us from possible pain. The boundaries they create help maintain a sense of control, but quietly block new experiences and growth. Underneath, there is often a resistance to positive change, an inner barrier made up of beliefs about what is safe, what is deserved, or what feels manageable. When these beliefs are left unexamined, self-sabotage not only continues but thrives.

Becoming aware of these patterns is the first step out of their shadow. Self-sabotage is common. Almost everyone uses it from time to time, often out of self-protection or habit rather than choice. Each act of procrastination, each moment spent chasing perfection, and each instance of avoiding discomfort can be an invitation to ask, "What am I really protecting myself from?"

Recognizing the subtle disguises of self-sabotage can begin to loosen their grip, stirring curiosity and hope that more fulfilling possibilities are waiting just beyond the safe territory of the familiar.

The Mask of Self-Deprecation

The mind can work in surprising ways to keep hope and happiness just out of reach. Someone sitting across from a glowing opportunity might still shrink back, caught up in worries and fears that seem almost impossible to brush away. There is no shortage of ambition, yet stepping forward can feel dangerous. Comfort zones, even when cramped, echo with a sense of safety. Growth asks adults to leave behind familiar roles and take on the unpredictability of change. That prospect stirs up inner resistance, not always loud, but steady enough to slow progress.

A key part of this resistance grows from beliefs about deserving love or success. Many adults bump into thoughts like, "Why should good things happen for me?" or "If I succeed, it won't last."

These ideas don't always sound harsh or dramatic. Sometimes, they slip in quietly, even at moments of achievement, softening excitement with doubt. At work or at home, a person might hear a compliment and instantly swat it away, cracking a joke or diverting attention to their shortcomings. "I only got lucky," someone might say during a celebration. The words sound light, even charming, but beneath them sits uncertainty about self-worth.

This sense of undeserving nudges people to create self-defeating stories about their talents and relationships. If you grew up hearing that mistakes brought disappointment or that pride was dangerous, you might grow to distrust praise or fear letting others down. These beliefs do not just live inside the mind; they shape daily actions. For example, someone fears being "found out" if they try for a promotion. The worry is not only about being unqualified but about falling short of expectations and feeling exposed. Rather than face possible disappointment, it feels easier to avoid the challenge altogether.

There is often a link between these beliefs and the need to control the outcome. When someone holds back from aiming higher or investing in friendships, there is a sense of: "If I keep my hopes low and don't try, I can't be disappointed if things go wrong." This way of shrinking ambitions appears to protect from hurtful surprises, but it actually limits growth. It is a kind of bargain; the person remains safe from pain, but also safe from joy and connection.

Self-sabotage does not always announce itself. Sometimes, it looks like humility, friendliness, or even wisdom. Someone who quips about always coming in second or makes light of their own success appears likable and self-aware. They might say, "Don't worry, I mess things up all the time," or "I'm not nearly as talented as you think." Humor shields them from others' expectations and, at the same time, from their own anxieties about failing. People who cling to humility in this way often think they are simply staying grounded. Yet this habit keeps them from truly accepting compliments, trying new things, and owning their strengths.

These defense strategies seem harmless, even virtuous, on the surface. Society praises humility and warns against arrogance, so minimizing one's abilities can feel like the right thing to do. However, there is a hidden cost. When you laugh off a genuine victory or hide your abilities, you also reinforce the idea that you don't deserve more. This loop strengthens feelings of insecurity and cements self-limiting beliefs. The longer someone avoids new opportunities or resists enjoying success, the harder it becomes to break these old habits.

Patterns of self-sabotage become a form of comfort, even when they stir up unease. Adults might pass on a new friendship, decline a chance to pursue a hobby, or avoid constructive feedback at work. They stay in situations that feel "safe" but unfulfilling, telling themselves that risk isn't worth the trouble. Over time, the habit of holding back becomes the path of least resistance. Success and belonging seem reserved for someone else.

These choices come with emotional consequences. In the quiet moments after a missed opportunity or an awkward joke, guilt and regret start to surface. The same thoughts that urged someone to play small now turn against them: "Why didn't I try?" or "I always do this to myself." The relief of avoiding danger is soon replaced by frustration with one's own actions. This cycle can be painful. Adults want to grow and find joy, but their own guarded choices keep pushing these things farther away. After a string of self-sabotaging moments, the emotional weight grows harder to ignore. Feelings of disappointment and self-criticism start to accumulate, becoming patterns that are difficult to break. Even when someone understands what is happening, it takes courage and clarity to start changing these hidden habits.

Recognizing the ways we protect ourselves, even when those habits hurt more than help, opens the door to change. It won't always be easy, and old fears will likely show up again, but awareness gives us power. With each small step toward honesty about our inner resistance and self-limiting beliefs, we create space for new habits, fresh opportunities, and real growth. This chapter is just the beginning; armed with insight and a bit of courage, we can start rewriting the stories we tell ourselves and move closer to the success and happiness we truly deserve.

Unmask the Moment

- When you think about your own habits, which patterns feel like they quietly hold you back—procrastination, perfectionism, avoidance, or something else?

- What emotions usually show up when you delay or avoid something important? Fear, doubt, or maybe a need to feel safe?

- Can you recall a time when you avoided an opportunity that could have helped you grow? What belief or worry kept you from moving forward?

- How do you typically respond to compliments or success? Do you accept them with gratitude, or do you minimize them like the examples in this chapter?

- Which of your daily behaviors might be protecting you from discomfort but also keeping you from joy or progress?

- How might faith—prayer, reflection, or scripture—help you face the inner barriers that lead to self-sabotage?

- What is one small, courageous step you can take this week to challenge a pattern that has been limiting your growth?

Chapter Two
Origins of Self-Sabotage

"**I**'m just going to mess this up again," Lisa whispered to herself, staring at the email draft she hadn't sent in weeks. Every time she thought about hitting "send," a rush of doubt flooded her: What if they reject her idea? What if she's not cut out for this?

Years before, those fears had taken root quietly, like seeds planted long ago, growing into a tangled web she couldn't quite explain. It wasn't just about fear of failure; it was something deeper, a mix of old hurts and voices that told her she wasn't enough. Sometimes, those voices made her pull back just when things were going well, as if protecting herself from disappointment before it arrived.

But what if those feelings weren't only about past pain or low confidence? What if there was more beneath the surface, something both psychological and spiritual, shaping the way we hold ourselves back? The struggle isn't always clear-cut; sometimes the hardest battles happen inside, where memories, beliefs, and faith overlap.

Where did these self-defeating patterns begin? How do early wounds shape our choices today? How might understanding both the mind and spirit help untangle the knots keeping us stuck? It's less about blame and more about discovering hidden roots, so that new growth, grounded in truth and compassion, becomes possible. Let's dig in!

Early Wounds and False Core Beliefs

Many people find themselves stuck in habits that seem to work against their own best interests. They may turn down exciting opportunities, push away people who care, or settle for less than they truly want. These are not just random mistakes. At the center of these self-sabotaging patterns are deep psychological wounds and spiritual struggles that begin early in life, combining messages picked up from painful relationships with false spiritual narratives about identity and worth.

Growing up in homes where love or acceptance was inconsistent plants the seeds of insecurity. When someone important withholds affection or abandons a child emotionally, the child looks for reasons why. Unable to imagine that the problem lies outside themselves, they absorb blame. This may sound like, "If I were lovable, my dad would have stayed," or "If I were better, my mother wouldn't be disappointed in me." These false beliefs burrow deep, quietly shaping the way a person understands relationships and themselves.

Over time, these internalized messages set the stage for adulthood filled with invisible barriers. Take the example of Lisa, who never felt sure of her mother's care. As an adult, she dates someone kind and stable, but as intimacy grows, so does her anxiety. Every compliment feels suspicious, every loving gesture an accident. She ends the relationship when it starts to feel too close, believing it's only a matter of time before she gets left. Her self-sabotage is not a conscious choice. Deep down, the old wound of rejection acts like an alarm, warning her never to trust fully or hope too much.

Sometimes the voices within tell us we are not enough. Mark has worked for years at a job he secretly dislikes, longing for something more. His boss finally offers a promotion, but Mark shrugs it off. Unseen by his colleagues is the "truth" Mark believes about himself: Good things are for other people. If he took the new role, he might disappoint everyone, prove himself a fake, and lose everything. He withdraws, protecting himself from the pain he imagines, while never realizing that the root of his hesitation is a story written long ago, by people who failed to see his value.

Underlying these stories is the reality that false core beliefs form quietly, through repetitive experiences and subtle messages. Psychologists note that children need consistent affirmation to develop a secure sense of worth. When that is missing, or when criticism overshadows encouragement, the mind searches for explanations. "I'm not good enough," "Nothing ever works out for me," or "If I show my true self, I'll be rejected." These ideas stick, fed by both memory and fear. Without careful examination, they become lenses through which every event is filtered.

Within a Christian perspective, there is another layer to this problem. Scripture teaches that each person is created with infinite value and purpose. Yet the experience of rejection or unworthiness works like a spiritual deception, a voice twisting the truth of God's love into a lie. Where God says, "You are my beloved," the wound whispers, "You are disposable." The battle is more than emotional; it is spiritual, pushing people to accept less and doubt more. Without the truth, lies take root and grow.

Spotting self-sabotage empowers change. When an unhelpful belief like "I'll never be enough" surfaces, challenge it with both psychological wisdom and faith. Affirm your strengths, remember moments when you succeeded or were loved, and recall what God says about your value. For example, replace the thought, "I am not good enough," with "I was made for more, and my worth is not up for debate." Rooting new truths deeply requires practice, patience, and compassion toward yourself.

Examining these patterns is not about blame or shame. It is an invitation to look curiously and kindly at the stories shaping your life. While early wounds and false beliefs create fertile ground for self-sabotage, they rarely account for everything.

The Role of Emotional Injury

Childhood shapes so much of how a person sees themselves and the world. Early experiences with parents or caregivers build the foundation for trust, self-worth, and emotional safety. When those relationships are supportive, a child learns that mistakes are not the end of the world, and they are accepted even when they fail. But when emotional wounds come from loneliness, criticism, harsh discipline, or neglect, a deep ache can settle inside. These early relational injuries plant seeds of doubt, shame, or fear. Over time, they grow into false beliefs such as "I'm never good enough" or "I must always stay on guard."

Some of these hurts are chronic, stretching across many years, and others are sharp, rooted in a single painful moment such as a public failure, experiencing severe punishment, or being let down by someone trusted. In a sense, very traumatic. Trauma isn't always dramatic or violent. Sometimes, it hides in ordinary moments: a parent's icy silence, a friend's betrayal, or words spoken in anger. Each leaves a mark, shaping the invisible scripts people live by. These injuries often linger beneath awareness, quietly coloring how someone reacts to challenges, relationships, or opportunities.

As adults, responses to these old wounds may not make sense at first. A person might avoid new growth or opportunities, not out of laziness or lack of desire, but because the memory of failure still burns deeply. They become experts in sidestepping risks, predicting catastrophe even when there is little reason to worry. This reaction sometimes provides a false sense of control, especially for someone who grew up feeling powerless or overlooked. Instead of feeling vulnerable and waiting for disappointment, they choose to end things on their own terms. The cycle becomes self-protective, even if it brings regret and missed chances.

Common reactions to unresolved trauma include avoidance, self-blame, and impulsivity. Avoidance shows up in the person who avoids applying for a job or joining social gatherings, convincing themselves it's better not to try than to risk failing. Self-blame can become a constant, silent companion, whispering that every setback is proof of personal weakness.

Trauma's influence burrows deep, often bypassing conscious thought. Habits and reactions build up over time, operating almost like background music, familiar, persistent, and nearly impossible to tune out. These coping patterns can become ingrained, slipping quietly into the routine of daily life. Because of this, breaking free can feel like trying to silence a song that has played for years. People might not realize certain choices, such as procrastinating on important projects, lashing out during conflict, or accepting less than they deserve in relationships, are connected to wounds from the past.

Recognizing these hidden influences is the first step towards change. Healing requires courage and honesty, but it does not have to happen alone.

Faith-based approaches can offer powerful tools for growth and recovery. Prayer, personal reflection, and forgiveness, both of oneself and others, can invite healing into wounded places.

Naming trauma does not mean letting it define the future. Instead, it opens a pathway to freedom, guiding each person towards healthier choices and relationships. Even as these practical strategies foster healing, it's important to realize that the struggle is not always limited to the mind or heart alone. Sometimes, other forces seem to press in—temptations, moments of discouragement, and subtle spiritual battles—that make breaking free even harder. These influences can deepen the patterns begun by trauma, making the process of change feel like a spiritual struggle as much as an emotional one, and the self-sabotaging behavior rears its head.

Spiritual Warfare

Sometimes, self-sabotage feels like a puzzle with pieces that don't quite fit. A voice inside whispers self-doubt while old wounds ache and spiritual heaviness clouds good intentions. Temptation and spiritual attack shape this battleground in ways that are subtle and confusing, weaving through emotions and thoughts that already feel raw from past pain. Psychology explains how hurt from the past may linger in beliefs and reactions. Christianity suggests that these emotional "open doors" can make a person more vulnerable to spiritual influences that aim to pull them away from hope, purpose, and truth.

Spiritual warfare, as Christians often describe it, frames daily struggles not just as psychological battles but as moments where unseen forces are hard at work. Self-sabotaging thoughts or actions can feel like everyday stress or low confidence, yet can also be seen as attempts to hold someone back from their God-given calling. Spiritual temptation isn't always a dramatic urge to do something obviously wrong. Often, it wears the face of self-doubt, discouragement, or a haunting sense of worthlessness. This overlap with psychological triggers makes it tricky to recognize whether a thought like "I'll never be enough" is only a learned response or a subtle push by a spiritual adversary.

For example, imagine someone who, anytime they try something new, hears the persistent message: "You'll fail, why bother starting?" This could echo a childhood memory of embarrassment or criticism, but, for Christians, it might also be a spiritual attack designed to stop them from using their abilities for good. The enemy, as described in scripture, loves to twist the knife in those fragile, unhealed places, making the fight feel lonely and impossible. In another case, consider a person almost at the finish line: a big job interview is tomorrow, or a cherished goal seems in reach. An anxious voice urges, "Maybe it's safer to wait, you're probably not ready." On the surface, this looks like rational caution. Underneath, though, it might be spiritual discouragement, using the language of fear to nudge the person away from courage and progress. These examples highlight how spiritual sabotage hides behind the mask of mental habits, disguising deeper motives in ordinary feelings. Untangling these threads requires honest reflection and spiritual wisdom, since the lines between inner pain and spiritual opposition rarely appear sharply drawn.

Spotting spiritual sabotage in daily life takes self-compassion and a willingness to look deeper without judgment or shame. People who have experienced deep hurt are not weak or flawed for having open doors. The best defense is gentle self-awareness. Watch for recurring thoughts or temptations that always arise when hope builds or purpose draws near. Notice if discouragement feels heavier than the moment warrants, or if familiar negative scripts return with uncanny timing. Allow space to consider a spiritual dimension; refusing to dismiss its role keeps more tools available for healing and growth. Blending spiritual discernment with psychological understanding works best because self-sabotage often has roots in both. Healing requires attending to wounds, but also refusing to let unseen influences define the future.

Imagine Lisa, who dreams of starting a small business. On the morning she plans to register her company, she's hit with a flood of anxiety: "You're not meant for this. You'll embarrass yourself." Her chest tightens, and she almost closes her laptop. She pauses, recognizes the thought as both an old fear and possibly a spiritual attack. Taking a deep breath, she offers up a brief prayer, asking God for courage and clarity. She remembers the verse that says, "God did not give us a spirit of fear, but of power." Repeating it softly, she opens the registration page again. With shaking hands, she fills in her details, one step, then another. The internal battle is fierce, but as she acts, a sense of calm and strength begins to settle in. The sabotaging thought loses its grip, and a quiet hope takes root. In that moment, Lisa feels both the freedom of letting go of old limitations and the deep encouragement that, spiritually and psychologically, she has begun a real change.

Early wounds, deep emotional pain, and even spiritual struggles work together to trip us up. We can start to spot those tricky self-sabotaging habits when they show up. Recognizing where these patterns come from, whether from past hurts, false beliefs, or spiritual attacks, gives us real power to break free. It means we're no longer stuck blaming ourselves or feeling alone in the fight. With a mix of kindness toward ourselves, practical steps, and faith, we can challenge old lies and choose new paths. The journey isn't always easy, but knowing what's behind the struggle helps us step forward with hope, courage, and the belief that lasting change is possible.

From Sabotage to Self-Love

- What trauma or wounds from your early days do you think you still carry?

- What fallacious core belief do you think impedes your progress and is recurrent in your day-to-day and professional engagements?

- When you notice your self-sabotaging behavior, habits, and practices kick in, what emotions dominate the mood and action? Fear, shame, doubt, or something else?

- What physical cues indicate that your self-sabotaging instincts are stirring up? (e.g., tension, anxiety, fatigue)

- What reactionary impulses and actions do you resort to most often? (e.g., avoidance, self-blame, tantrums, or rage fits)

- When facing self-doubt or fear, what spiritual practices help you recognize your true value and purpose?

- What truths about you can you use as leverage to help you identify, control, and then eliminate your self-sabotaging patterns and habits?

Chapter Three
Breaking the Silence

"I can handle it on my own," I told myself for years, brushing off the nagging feeling that something was holding me back. Admitting there might be a problem felt like admitting failure, something I just wasn't ready to do. It's not just me; many adults struggle with opening up about self-sabotage because of the weight of shame and the fear that they'll be seen as weak or incapable. We live in a world that prizes strength and success, so confessing to patterns that trip us up feels risky, even dangerous.

Let us explore how stigma and shame keep the conversation quiet, how society often normalizes behaviors that actually hold us back, and how internal fears make vulnerability feel impossible. You'll also see how denial and defensiveness act like shields, blocking honest self-awareness. Understanding these barriers is the first step toward breaking through silence and starting a more honest relationship with yourself.

Facing External Barriers

Many adults feel an irresistible urge to hide their self-sabotaging habits. Stigma and shame turn these private struggles into things no one wants to admit. In a world where productivity and self-control are prized, confessing to self-created setbacks feels like announcing a personal defeat. The barriers to honesty don't just exist in the mind;

they're woven tightly into the social fabric and reinforced by the ways we talk about, joke about, or overlook everyday self-sabotage.

Admitting to self-sabotage isn't easy. It often sounds like confessing to a flaw or a personal weakness. Adults fear being judged as unreliable, lazy, or just failing at "adulting." For someone who repeatedly misses deadlines or spends nights lost in distractions online, opening up about the real reasons behind their actions can feel like stepping into a spotlight that exposes all their insecurities.

That fear comes with heavy shame. Shame whispers that these habits aren't just mistakes, but evidence of something embarrassing or defective in the person themselves. Shame convinces people that while others might occasionally mess up, their own patterns are something to hide. This swirl of self-judgment keeps people silent. They tell themselves, "No one else struggles like this." That silence also sends the message that these problems don't deserve help, or, worse, that help wouldn't change anything.

Stigma doesn't just affect individuals internally. It's a powerful social force. People worry about being seen as undisciplined or "not serious" if they admit to self-sabotage, especially in careers or communities where achievement is the measure of worth. The result is a pattern of self-censorship. If someone is known for missing opportunities, they risk being left out of projects or promotions. Fear of labels makes people hide their struggles from friends and colleagues, locked away behind casual jokes or polite excuses.

This creates a cycle: the less people talk, the more isolated they feel. When they carry struggles in silence, it becomes even harder to imagine reaching out for support. The stigma creates a wall between the person and the help they need.

If stigma and shame push adults into secrecy, society's tendency to normalize self-sabotage adds an extra invisible layer. Many self-sabotaging habits are brushed off as quirks or harmless behaviors.

It's easy to hear someone laugh about being a "night owl" who can't get anything done before noon. Or the professional who delays important work but blames it on loving the creative pressure of deadlines. These are ways to reframe self-defeating habits as parts of a personality rather than signals that something is wrong.

This normalization is everywhere. People joke online about "doom-scrolling" instead of sleeping or doing the chores they've put off. Friends commiserate over another binge-watching session that wrecked their plans. Instead of addressing the behaviors, society often offers a wink and a nudge, reinforcing a culture where everyone's hidden battles remain unspoken. These outside attitudes work their way into the individual's mind. Growing up hearing parents say, "I've always been like this," or watching peers joke away their missed goals, adults adopt the belief that their own struggles are normal, inevitable, or simply not worth mentioning. When the world seems to shrug at these patterns, it's easy to downplay their impact. Instead of reflecting seriously, people rationalize their behavior: "Everyone procrastinates," "That's just my style." The cycle deepens as individuals avoid looking closely at the roots of their self-sabotage.

Family, friends, and co-workers often reinforce this silence. Support systems can be quick to minimize concerns, offering reassurance without challenging the pattern: "Don't worry, it's not a big deal." This can be comforting but ultimately discourages real self-reflection or change.

Beneath layers of social pressure, shame, and minimization lies an even tougher obstacle: the fear that real honesty will expose the vulnerable parts of ourselves that we want to keep hidden. Stigma and normalization may be outward forces, but the internal dread of showing weakness is deeply personal. It's not just about fearing what others will think; it's the panic that, once acknowledged, secret struggles could confirm the worst fears about ourselves.

This fear is what makes silence around self-sabotaging habits so hard to break. Until someone can look past the noise of stigma and the comfort of normalization, the anxiety about revealing hidden struggles grows. For many adults, it's easier to laugh, minimize, or remain silent, anything to avoid that moment of vulnerability. The result is a powerful combination of influences, working in unison, that keeps the conversation about self-sabotage locked behind closed doors.

The Internal Battle

When society casts stubborn shadows of shame over mistakes, and when those around us celebrate only success, an invisible pressure grows beneath the surface. It's a force that urges people to keep quiet about their flaws and hardships, even as these experiences stack up behind closed doors. Many adults, feeling the pinch of these expectations, turn their discomfort inward and clamp down on anything that might hint at failure. These deep-seated norms, once fully accepted as truth, start to shape the way people see themselves. This is how fear of vulnerability lodges itself in the mind, quiet, heavy, and persistent.

Fear of vulnerability acts like a watchdog, forever on alert to threats to one's reputation or sense of self-worth. Instead of simply deciding whether to be honest about mistakes, many adults find themselves up against a wall of silent terror: What if someone really saw who I am underneath it all? The idea of exposing self-sabotage, whether it's procrastination, avoidance, or repeated stumbles, hits nerves grown raw from years of trying to meet other people's and their own unspoken standards. There's a risk that by admitting to these private trips and falls, others might judge, reject, or quietly write them off as not quite good enough. Even a tiny slip can feel like a landslide.

This fear isn't just some imaginary bogeyman. It runs on real consequences, fueled by past experiences and cultural messaging.

When someone's dignity, career, or relationships feel like they're on the line, the urge to hide grows even stronger. Images come to mind of a reliable coworker who starts turning in projects late, again and again, but always has an excuse ready. Every missed deadline is covered with a joke or a story. They can't bring themselves to explain what's really going on: a fear of disappointing others, or perhaps paralyzing perfectionism. To everyone else, it just seems like a case of disorganization or laziness, but beneath the surface sits a dread of being unmasked. If anyone knew about their struggle, they worry it would stain their reputation and affect their future.

Similar patterns emerge at home. Imagine a partner who refuses to talk about mounting tension or drifting apart, no matter how many hints are dropped. They shield themselves from hard conversations about intimacy, money, or unmet needs, insisting there's nothing wrong. The silence isn't uncaring, it's armor! By not speaking, they hope to sidestep embarrassment, avoid conflict, and protect the fragile image of being a "good" spouse. There's a persistent internal whisper: Admitting struggle could make it all fall apart, so better to pretend it doesn't exist.

These examples reveal the secret: vulnerability threatens people because it demands that they surrender their mask and let others peek behind it. When adults consider revealing any deep hurt or recurring failing, a mental dialogue unfolds. Thoughts arise such as, "If I never let this slip, no one can judge me," or "Bringing this up will make things awkward, and it's not worth the risk." Each defensive thought tightens the inner lock, making it less likely anyone will reach out for help or compassion. This strategy creates a temporary sense of safety, but it also breeds long-term loneliness and self-doubt.

Courage in the face of vulnerability doesn't require grand gestures.

Courageous conversations rarely happen in great leaps. More often, they grow from quiet, careful steps. Each time someone expresses a little more of their truth, they shrink the hold fear has on them.

Gradual honesty lays down a path toward believing that acceptance is possible, from others and from themselves.

These inner barriers don't arise solely because people fear others' judgment. The mind itself works hard to protect against pain, building defenses that can become habits. Internal walls gain strength, promoted not only by outside pressures but also by the mental routines that convince someone they're safer staying silent. The complexities of these internal guardians are worth untangling; the story behind those walls is both more ordinary and more powerful than it first appears.

Denial and Defensiveness

Even after facing the fear of vulnerability, adults can find themselves slipping into habits that keep the truth hidden from themselves and others. Denial and defensiveness aren't just negative words; they're everyday tools the mind uses to avoid pain. These responses happen fast and often go unnoticed. You might catch yourself avoiding an uncomfortable reflection on your own actions, or feeling a prick of annoyance when someone points a finger at your mistakes. Most adults don't want to feel broken or blameworthy. Denial and defensiveness help maintain that tougher, cleaner self-image, even at the expense of growth.

Denial is slippery. Sometimes it simply means forgetting a pattern that hurts, or weaving reality into a narrative that feels more manageable. Think of someone who, after missing several deadlines at the office, insists they "do their best work under pressure." The mounting stress, the last-minute panic, these might point to deeper avoidance behaviors, but denial smooths over the pattern. In relationships, denial pops up when someone claims, "We never really fight," despite a constant simmer of unresolved tension. It's easy and tempting because self-awareness can sting. The mind skips over discomfort to protect itself, and suddenly, responsibility for self-sabotage vanishes from view.

Defensiveness is just as familiar. Where denial blocks recognition, defensiveness arms itself against anything that hints at personal fault.

After a partner voices concern about emotional distance, an adult might reply, "I'm just tired from work; not everyone needs to talk all the time." In friendships, someone asked about flaky behavior may bristle: "Well, I'm busy, at least I'm not constantly checking my phone when we're together." At work, criticism melts into retorts like, "It's not my fault, the instructions were never clear," or "Everyone's behind, not just me." Each defensive move shields the ego. Rather than absorb feedback, the adult reflexively explains it away, blames outside forces, or shrinks the problem until it disappears.

Both denial and defensiveness provide relief from uncomfortable truths. They avoid guilt, keep the narrative of being a good person intact, and let adults sidestep shame. However, these short-term comforts chain people to their self-sabotaging cycles. The office procrastinator never learns what is really dragging their performance down. Someone trapped in defensive ruts at home never sees how stunted communication limits intimacy. Change doesn't start until someone begins to notice these shields and then gently lowers them, if only for a moment.

You don't have to rip the walls down in a single day. Being honest about the small stories you tell yourself is the first move toward freedom.

Lila often arrived late to meetings and snapped at coworkers who teased her about it. Her typical thought: "I'm slammed with work, and everyone else runs late too." After trying this exercise, Lila paused the next time a coworker gently pointed out her lateness. She wrote down her knee-jerk thought: "It's not my fault, they're picking on me." Later, reviewing her notes, she realized she felt embarrassed to stand out in a group but had always masked it with irritation and blame. When she practiced taking a breath and responding, "Thank you for letting me know, I'll work on it," she felt vulnerable, but also lighter. Lila wasn't perfect, but admitting this small flaw let her move forward.

Spotting these patterns takes practice but opens the door for genuine change. Denial and defensiveness lose power the moment they're named and understood. The next time you feel the urge to explain, dismiss, or avoid, pause. Your real growth begins right there.

Now that we've uncovered the many walls built by stigma, shame, normalization, and our own defenses, it's clear why admitting self-sabotage feels so tough. But understanding these barriers is the first step toward breaking them down. When we recognize how fear and myths keep us silent, we can begin to challenge those stories we tell ourselves and others. By taking small, honest steps, whether writing in a journal, sharing with a trusted friend, or simply pausing before reacting, we open the door to real change. Moving past denial and defensiveness isn't about being perfect; it's about giving ourselves permission to be human, mess up, and grow. The path forward may feel scary at times, but each moment of courage brings us closer to freedom from the silence that holds us back.

Bringing Down the Walls

- Whenever you take the small steps to acknowledge and deal with self-sabotage, what feelings, apprehensions, fears, or shame surface?

- Has the desire to appear "strong" influenced your willingness to admit struggles? If yes, what societal expectations do you think you have succumbed to the most?

- What is your most noticeable go-to act or habit that takes charge whenever your minimizing or normalizing self-sabotaging instincts kick in? Which ones of them are so obvious that even your peers or close ones will point them out? You can even ask your friends.

- When has denial or defensiveness cost you the biggest opportunity, and how did it prevent you from seeing the real reasons behind a repeated mistake or behavior?

- In what areas does the fear of vulnerability dictate your life the most: relationships, work, or personal goals? If you have to begin somewhere and start calling it out, what area is the best to start?

- What small step could you take now, today, that can facilitate practicing honesty about a self-sabotaging habit?

Chapter Four
Self-Sabotage in the Bible and Modern Life

Most people will sabotage their own success at some point, often without even realizing it. Studies show that nearly 70% of people struggle with self-defeating behaviors that hold them back from reaching their full potential. Whether it's pride, fear, or unchecked emotions, these hidden forces quietly chip away at what could have been, creating a cycle that's hard to break.

This isn't just a modern problem; it's been happening for thousands of years. The stories we tell about heroes and leaders reveal something surprising: even the strongest people can be their own worst enemies. When giants fall, it usually isn't because of outside enemies but because they let internal struggles control their choices. And those moments of self-sabotage don't just change the course of their lives; they ripple out, affecting everyone around them.

Understanding how this works helps us see our own challenges in a new light. It allows us to spot the warning signs before pride or fear takes over and teaches us why breaking free from these patterns requires more than just willpower. This chapter digs into these hidden battles, showing that the path to true growth starts when we learn to face ourselves honestly and make different choices, even when it's hard.

Samson's Folly and King Saul's Insecurity

Picture the heroes of old, not as distant legends or perfect saints, but as people facing battles much like our own. The Bible gives us stories where giants of faith, people called and empowered for greatness, still found ways to trip themselves up. Self-sabotage, at its heart, isn't just about failing to accomplish something. In biblical terms, it usually springs from flaws within: pride, insecurity, reckless choices, or unchecked emotions. When these giants fell, it almost never happened because a stronger enemy bested them. Usually, they crumbled from the inside out. We resonate with these stories because they feel familiar. They reflect our own inner struggles: those moments when we ignore better judgment, give in to emotion, or let personal fears rule over what we know to be right.

Samson's life reads almost like an ancient superhero tale. Blessed from birth with extraordinary strength, he was marked out as someone who could inspire awe and lead his people. But instead of taking the steady path, his pride pushed him to believe nothing could really touch him. Time and again, Samson tested the boundaries, toying with danger and treating his gifts like unbreakable armor. He married Philistine women despite the risks, got involved in trouble he could have easily avoided, and seemed to treat his calling as something meant more for personal thrill than real purpose.

One of the most vivid pictures of Samson's self-sabotage comes from his relationship with Delilah. He knew there were people out to get him, but rather than step back, he continued to play with fire. Delilah pressed him for the secret of his strength; instead of putting a stop to it, Samson taunted, teased, and finally, sure he couldn't truly be defeated, told her what made him powerful. It's easy to see pride at work: the confidence that his strength would always be there, combined with the thrill of the risk he kept courting. As a result, Delilah betrayed him, his hair was cut, and his strength was gone.

Blind and humiliated, Samson ended up entertaining his enemies, paying a staggering price for mistakes that were not destiny, but decisions he made over and over. His story shouts a warning: no matter how gifted, letting ego and impulse lead can undo even the strongest person.

It's not just about physical strength or obvious recklessness. Sometimes, what brings giants down is harder to spot from the outside. Insecurity can be quiet, festering beneath the surface until it shapes every choice. King Saul stands as a powerful example of this more subtle, but equally devastating form of self-sabotage. When Saul first became king, he was humble and unsure, but he had genuineness and promise. People noticed him, looked to him for leadership, and God's favor rested on him.

Things began to unravel when Saul started watching others' applause more than his calling. As David appeared on the scene, Saul saw a new hero rising and felt the old sinking weight of inadequacy. He became jealous, imagining threats where there were none, and started making decisions that were defensive and desperate. Saul's insecurity pushed him to cling to power at all costs. He ignored God's instructions, tried to outmaneuver his rivals, and even hunted David, who had done him no harm. The more he tried to control things, the more they slipped away. His anxiety dissolved his sense of perspective, alienating him from loyal friends, his own family, and the God who had once set him apart. Saul's final years were marked by depression and spiritual darkness, his potential hijacked by fears he couldn't admit or overcome. In him, we see how leadership can be hollowed out, not by a single mistake, but by the ongoing erosion that comes from self-doubt, envy, and losing trust in your own path.

The pattern is hard to ignore. These stories act as a sort of mirror. For modern readers, the details may change, our "gifts" and "battles" look different, but the core struggles carry forward into our families, workplaces, and hearts. Self-sabotage rarely arrives all at once.

Sometimes it's the sum of tiny, impulsive choices, risk-taking for its own sake, or yielding over and over to anxious thoughts. Other times, it's the moment a burst of anger or an unchecked emotion tips the balance.

Even as the stories shift from pride and insecurity to other forms, like anger, the thread continues; sometimes it only takes a single careless moment to reroute a destiny that was poised for greatness. Without naming the next story, the journey moves into how powerful emotions, left unmeasured, could derail even the most faithful.

Moses and Anger

Sometimes the greatest threats to strong leadership don't come from outside but from hidden fractures beneath the surface, places where pride evolves into insecurity and erupts through unexpected cracks. The story of Moses, one of the most revered leaders in biblical history, becomes especially revealing here. He had survived rebellion, navigated the turmoil of liberating an entire nation, and spoken with God for guidance time after time. Yet, despite this near-legendary résumé, Moses' journey unraveled at a crucial moment because of something less obvious than pride, an emotion boiling up underneath, left unchecked until it changed the course of everything.

Moses reached a breaking point in Numbers 20, standing before a parched, impatient crowd. God gave him clear instructions: speak to the rock, and water would flow. Instead, Moses, fueled by anger and frustration, struck the rock not once, but twice. Water poured out, meeting the people's immediate need. The miracle happened anyway, but the cost was immense: Moses was barred from entering the very land he had spent decades trying to reach. One moment, one overwhelming emotion, and a destiny reshaped forever.

What happened here wasn't just a flash of temper. Moses' anger masked deeper struggles, weariness from relentless demands, disappointment over Israel's ceaseless complaints, perhaps the burden of feeling inadequate to lead a stubborn people. The act of hitting the rock was more than disobedience; it laid bare the cluttered, complicated world inside a leader's heart. With one impulsive act, years of obedience faded, and his legacy changed from one of ultimate triumph to one marked by one painful misstep.

Unchecked emotions don't discriminate by age or wisdom. Even Moses, the man who "spoke to God as a friend," tripped over his inner tumult in his final act of public ministry. Leaders like him are often tempted to believe their titles or experience make them immune to basic human weaknesses, but this story insists otherwise. When pressure mounts and expectations soar, frustration or hurt can override years of training and cloud the clearest of visions. This is as true around a modern boardroom table as it was by the ancient rock in the desert.

The consequences of self-sabotage ripple outward. Moses' anger didn't just affect him; it affected the community's trajectory, the way future generations spoke of him, and even the intimate relationship he'd enjoyed with God. Consider how often a harsh word or rash decision, a slammed door, an accusatory email, a hasty social media post, undercuts hard-won respect. The trust of followers gets chipped away, opportunities close, and relationships fray in ways that can take years to mend.

Even the most dutiful person risks undoing years of steady progress in a moment of unchecked emotion. Maybe it's a coach who lashes out and loses the support of the team, or a manager who lets irritation fuel a dismissive comment that stifles initiative and trust. These aren't just character flaws; they become defining moments that change stories and shape legacies.

Ignoring the early warning signals—resentment simmering, fatigue quietly building, insecurity morphing into defensiveness—can cost more than immediate comfort or temporary control. Spiritual health erodes as pride convinces a person they don't need help, and relational connections weaken because vulnerability gives way to self-protection. Wisdom gives way to reaction, and the gap between intention and action grows wider.

The lesson emerging from Moses' example goes beyond just "control your anger." It's a call to self-awareness and humility, recognizing that the real hazards lie inside, not out there in the world. Leaders and followers alike need room to pause and name their emotions before they harden into damaging choices. Constructive change starts with one honest assessment, one brave admission of fear or frustration, and the willingness to make adjustments before the stakes get too high and before self-sabotaging behavior is irreversible.

Scripture quietly threads this theme throughout the stories of other figures, too. Saul's jealousy drives him to madness and ruin. Jonah's resentment leaves him alone under a withered vine. Even in the New Testament, hints of this pattern surface: Peter's fear leading to denial, for instance, or the doubts of Thomas shadowing hope. The faces and circumstances shift, but the core challenge remains: to meet the storms within as honestly as those without. The echo is clear for any age or context, unchecked emotions will always find a way to speak, often louder and more consequentially than words or intentions ever could.

Peter's Denial

Unchecked emotion does not disappear as the centuries pass; it finds new expressions in the lives of people who desperately want to do what is right but are ambushed by their own fears. The New Testament does not soften or ignore these human struggles. Among its stories, Peter's experience stands out as a stark portrait of self-sabotage that mirrors familiar themes: zeal undermined by anxiety, devotion toppled by overwhelming pressure.

Peter loved Jesus fiercely, sometimes leaping ahead when others hesitated. He was quick to speak, quick to act, and just as quick to stumble over his own good intentions. Jesus warned his disciples that a time of testing would come, and Peter brushed aside the danger. "Lord, I am ready to go with you to prison and to death," he said. His loyalty was sincere, but below the surface, deep fears waited. This set the stage for a crisis that would turn his world upside down.

When armed men came in the night to arrest Jesus, chaos filled the garden. The sense of safety vanished. Loyalty meant risk, maybe even death. Peter followed the soldiers and Jesus, moving closer to see what would happen. He entered the courtyard, lurking in the glow of a nearby fire. Shadows danced, and voices whispered. Peter's heart pounded. In a moment of raw honesty, the story does not paint Peter as a coward detached from his leader. He wavered on the edge, caught between devotion and the rising cold of fear that pressed in from all sides.

A servant girl looked closely at Peter and said, "This man was also with him." The accusation was simple, but the danger was real. Peter's first denial slipped out: "Woman, I do not know him." The words shocked even him. The tension peaked each time someone recognized him, forcing Peter further along the path of self-preservation. Another voice challenged him: "You also are one of them." His answer grew stronger: "Man, I am not." As the night wore on and the fire's light flickered, a third person insisted, "Certainly this man also was with him, for he too is a Galilean." Peter's fear won out entirely: "Man, I do not know what you are talking about." The sound of a rooster crowing ended the cycle, a sharp reminder of what Jesus had predicted.

Peter's denial was not just a slip of the tongue. It was a moment when the pressure of survival crashed against his desire to be faithful. Every ounce of pride drained away. He could not escape the truth. Luke's account describes this moment with clarity: "The Lord turned and looked at Peter." In that glance, all of Peter's bravado and promises crumbled. He left the courtyard and wept bitterly, grief pouring out as he faced his own failure.

This story captures what it feels like to lose sight of what matters under intense stress. In workplaces today, adults sometimes betray their values out of fear: someone keeps silent rather than stand up for a colleague, or agrees to something they know is wrong simply to protect themselves. The regret that follows is real, uncomfortable, and pushes people to reconsider who they are and what they want to become. Self-sabotage is always standing at the door!

For Peter, that night was not the end of his story. He did not deny his failure or try to hide from it. The pain of his self-sabotage forced him to face hard truths about his own weakness. Instead of retreating permanently, he allowed himself to be changed. When Jesus returned after the resurrection, he sought Peter out, not to shame him, but to restore him. The conversation beside the sea, with Jesus asking Peter three times, "Do you love me?" matched the pattern of his earlier denials. Each time, Peter responded with growing humility and honest love.

The aftermath of Peter's mistake became the ground for something new. He gained a deeper understanding of grace, became less quick to boast and judge, and was able to empathize with others who fell short. As Peter grew, he became a strong leader, his openness about failure helping others trust him. He broke the cycle of self-sabotage by refusing to let his worst moment define him forever.

Patterns of destructive fear and rashness do not just disappear, but they can be interrupted. Peter's story stands as both a warning and an encouragement. The cost of self-sabotage is real: broken trust, regret, and the need to repair relationships. But the story does not end there. When the aftermath is met with honesty and a willingness to change, personal and spiritual renewal are possible, not just for biblical giants but for anyone today who faces the pull of fear and regret.

Before the Fall Becomes Final

- Where in your life do you see patterns of self-sabotage—small choices or reactions that quietly work against what you say you want most?

- Samson treated his gifts as if they made him untouchable. In what ways might your strengths, talents, or past successes be tempting you to ignore warning signs or boundaries?

- Samson knew Delilah was dangerous, yet stayed anyway. What situations, relationships, or habits do you continue to entertain even though you sense the risk?

- King Saul's downfall grew from insecurity rather than obvious wrongdoing. Where does comparison or fear of being replaced influence your decisions or relationships?

- Saul watched others' applause more than his own calling. Whose approval do you find yourself quietly chasing, and how does that pursuit shape your behavior?

- Moses' anger erupted after long-term fatigue and frustration. What emotions have you been suppressing or "pushing through" that may be closer to the surface than you realize?

- Think about a recent moment where frustration or exhaustion led you to respond in a way you later regretted. What were the early warning signs you overlooked?

- What emotions, if left unchecked, are most likely to derail your integrity, faith, or relationships?

- What would it look like to pause earlier—to name your emotions honestly before they turn into decisions you cannot undo?

- Where might humility—asking for help, admitting weakness, slowing down—be the key to interrupting a cycle of self-sabotage in your life?

- What is one small, intentional adjustment you can make now to protect what matters most before pressure or emotion takes control?

- Finally, what truth about yourself is this chapter inviting you to face—not with shame, but with honesty and courage?

Chapter Five
Modern-Day Mirrors

Have you ever found yourself standing at a crossroads, knowing deep down that a choice you made is slowly unraveling the life you've worked so hard to build? Maybe it's a missed opportunity at work because you couldn't accept feedback, or a relationship drifting apart as mistrust quietly crept in. Sometimes, these moments sneak up on us—the small decisions, the silent doubts, the fears we try to hide even from ourselves. They grow into patterns we barely notice until suddenly, the consequences feel too big to ignore. What causes us to get in our own way like this, and why does it seem so hard to break free? These questions touch on struggles many of us face, often hidden behind smiles or excuses, leaving us wondering how we ended up here and if there's any hope for change.

Workplace Failures and Relationship Breakdowns

Walking into the office that morning, Bryan felt invincible. A celebrated manager, he had just launched an ambitious project he insisted would transform his team's image. When his assistant gently pointed out a flaw in the proposal, one that could spiral out of control if not fixed, Bryan dismissed her with a wave. Weeks passed, and murmurs grew about missed targets and client confusion. Co-workers raised valid concerns, but Bryan's confidence morphed into stubbornness. Instead of pausing to reassess, he doubled down, believing change would be a sign of weakness. When the project collapsed, taking two valuable clients with it, the fallout was swift. In the exit interview, his supervisor quietly noted, "We tried to help you see it, but you weren't listening." All along, Bryan's undoing had not been the project itself, but his unwillingness to heed feedback; his pride blocked the doorway to learning. He masked insecurity about being seen as weak with bravado, creating a vicious cycle that ended with a career setback he could no longer ignore.

The Power of Listening

Avoidable mistakes in professional environments rarely happen overnight. Consider Lila, a talented graphic designer, who once thrived on collaboration until she began to interpret suggestions as personal slights. Each critique pushed her deeper into defensiveness. She stopped sharing drafts, convinced co-workers were against her, using every small victory to bolster her sense of rightness. When a major contract went sideways because Lila refused to modify her designs, the client left for a rival firm. Management noticed the pattern: her refusal to trust the process, her inability to recognize collective wisdom over individual pride. Lila's self-sabotage took root in a fragile self-image. Wanting to prove her worth, she overlooked the simple truth that growth depends on learning from and working with others. The sting of rejection or criticism, for those who harbor unspoken fears of inadequacy, can turn every workplace into a minefield.

What Drives These Patterns

Patterns like Bryan's and Lila's unfold for reasons more complicated than mere stubbornness. Many individuals, shaped by earlier disappointments, quietly doubt their competence. Facing criticism, their minds leap to old pains, and defense mechanisms take over. Some push forward recklessly, others turn inward, tuning out the world to protect a bruised ego. The cycle becomes familiar: warning signs are downplayed, tension rises, and mistakes accumulate. Coworkers notice but stop offering help when they realize their words fall on deaf ears. The professional cost can include missed promotions, tarnished reputations, or even job loss, all stemming from the quiet force of pride or fear masquerading as self-assurance.

Self-Sabotage in Relationships

Similar patterns play out in the hidden corners of personal lives. When Angela and Milo first married, their evenings glowed with affection and long talks. Over the years, unresolved arguments left scars. Angela, carrying wounds from earlier betrayals, responded to Milo's questions with suspicion, even when he meant well. She began snooping through his messages, reading silence as rejection. Milo, confused and hurt, withdrew. Whenever conflict flared, Angela grew cold, refusing to talk or address the root of their troubles. These habits deepened over time, shaping their marriage into a fragile dance of distance and doubt. The more Angela acted on distrust, the more Milo pulled away, feeding the very fear she could never speak aloud. Eventually, their connection snapped, not because of one argument but from the quiet corrosion of repeated self-sabotage, each choice driven by the pain of old wounds and a desperate longing to feel secure.

The Cost of Disconnection

Friendships suffer in similar ways. Jordan and Leo shared everything for years, but when life changed, Leo found new success and spent less time together with Jordan, Jordan assumed the worst. Instead of congratulating his friend, he made offhand remarks and resented every missed call. Even when Leo reached out, Jordan replied curtly or declined invitations. What drove him wasn't malice but a deep-rooted belief that he would be abandoned, just as he'd often felt growing up. By acting out, pushing Leo away, Jordan created the very loneliness he dreaded. Their friendship quietly faded, proof that unchecked self-sabotage does more than ruin mood; it reshapes lives.

The Search for Relief

At every turn, these stories point to a more profound pattern. Most self-defeating behaviors sprout from hidden pain or unmet needs—often, a desire for recognition, protection, or love. Pride, distrust, and withdrawal don't arise in a vacuum; they bloom in the cracks left by disappointment and fear. People, unsure of how to heal, chase fleeting comfort instead, sometimes spiraling into activities that numb rather than mend. The urge for validation, the ache of insecurity, and the shadow of the past set the stage for choices that hurt more than help, quietly inviting other harmful escapes that promise relief but never deliver true healing.

Cycles of Addiction and Isolation

Hidden wounds sometimes linger beneath the surface, shaping choices and patterns in unexpected ways. For many, deep-seated pain creates an ache they cannot shake, a tension that demands relief. When familiar comforts like work or relationships no longer provide escape, some reach for substances, searching for numbness or a few hours of peace. What begins as a simple desire to avoid discomfort soon forms a desperate loop: relief gives way to guilt, guilt deepens the wound, and the craving returns stronger. In modern life, these cycles of addiction reveal not just personal struggle but a profound need to face and heal inner pain.

Addiction as a Mirror of Hurt

Sam once filled his days with ambition and a tight social circle. High school friends described him as quick to laugh, determined, and known for helping others. Yet home felt like walking on eggshells. His father's temper flashes left invisible bruises behind, teaching Sam to shrink from confrontation and bury distress inside. The pain accumulated year after year, hidden by a facade of smiles and achievements.

College brought more freedom but also new anxieties. When sleeplessness and panic attacks began to make classes impossible, Sam drank to quiet his mind. The initial comfort alcohol provided lasted only a few hours, quickly replaced by shame and an even deeper sense of despair. Rather than face the terror of failing, he hid, skipping lectures and dodging calls from worried friends. Attempts to quit evaporated under mounting pressure when he felt exposed or alone, and each relapse confirmed his worst fears that he was broken and beyond help.

The Pull of Isolation

Isolation reinforces addiction's grip. Kendra's story unfolds in different circumstances but echoes similar patterns. Growing up, she weathered the grief of losing her mother at ten and never found the words to express her feelings. Her father, overwhelmed and silent, offered practical support but little comfort. In her teens, Kendra experimented with pills for a sense of calm she never felt at home. She soon relied on them just to get through the day.

Kendra's friendships thinned as she drifted further from the world. She recognized the hurt she inflicted on herself and her relationships, but felt powerless to stop. Shame fed her loneliness and made reaching out all but impossible. Attempts to quit—countless, desperate, and solo—ended with overwhelming withdrawal symptoms and crushing self-doubt. Every failed effort reminded her of what she feared: that she deserved this pain and could not break free.

Cycles of Relapse and Reinforced Despair

Whether rooted in childhood trauma or profound grief, emotional wounds often lie at the heart of addiction. Substances seem to dull the ache or provide fleeting confidence, but the underlying hurt remains unaddressed. As people cycle between using and regretting, the notion of recovery grows ever more distant. Social ties fray when friends and family no longer know how to help or withdraw out of frustration. Professional setbacks follow as focus falters and energy disappears, deepening the feeling of falling behind in every aspect of life.

The reality is that cold-turkey attempts rarely succeed long-term, especially when the underlying emotional storms go unheeded. Quitting in isolation strips away hope. With no one to share burdens or guide through the hardest days, setbacks seem insurmountable. Without support, the simple act of reaching out feels dangerous, exposing vulnerabilities that shame has trained people to hide. Each failed attempt at sobriety builds the case for self-condemnation, locking addiction more tightly in place.

If addiction is often misunderstood as a lack of willpower, these stories reveal it as a tangled response to real and pressing emotional pain. Substances offer a short-term solution, but no lasting relief. Attempts to white-knuckle through withdrawal can become a test of endurance that overlooks the actual source of hurt. Treatment that focuses only on physical symptoms often fails, leading to repeated relapse.

Glimpses of Self-Awareness and Change

Even in the deepest habitual ruts, something shifts when pain and the longing for relief finally collide with a sense of tiredness, a wish that things could be different. Sometimes it is a quiet moment, alone on a bus or back in a childhood bedroom, where a small voice wonders if help might exist after all. Other times it is exhaustion, the kind that follows a final, fruitless attempt to get clean in secret.

In recognizing harmful patterns, seeing the link between relief and pain becomes the first vital flicker of hope. Through small acts of honesty or rare admissions to another person, those caught in addiction glimpse not only the possibility of healing but also the importance of genuine connection. What often starts in isolation can, with support and understanding, begin to open a door to lasting change. With every moment of awareness, the chance for something different takes root.

Recognizing Patterns and Choosing Change

Sarah's story began with a once-promising corporate career dimmed by her habit of sabotaging promotions and projects. She kept noticing her name was always missing from important advancement lists, even though her peers mentioned her talents. At first, she blamed the company culture, seeing others as more favored by management. But after an uncomfortable exit interview, where her supervisor gently pointed out her tendency to miss deadlines and avoid taking credit for collaborative efforts, Sarah felt something click. She saw that her pattern went way back, like not applying for scholarships in college, and hesitating to speak up even when she had good ideas. The recognition stung, but it brought relief. She was not unlucky; she was stuck in a groove she could change.

Sarah decided to treat her professional life more like a project she could manage. She wrote down moments she hesitated, noting how each was driven by fear of criticism or failure. Awareness helped her catch herself in the act, and she began speaking up in meetings, volunteering for challenging assignments, and openly claiming her successes when working with others. A supportive mentor at work met with her monthly, giving honest feedback and helping her set realistic goals. Over time, Sarah noticed her confidence growing, her work improving, and praise coming more consistently. That year, she earned her first promotion in six years. The realization that self-sabotage can be recognized and redirected, one new behavior at a time, became her turning point.

The Power of Naming the Pattern

For Kevin, self-sabotage showed up not in addiction or at work, but in his relationships. He had always been the type to pull away when things got intimate, finding minor flaws in partners or starting arguments just as closeness deepened. After the sudden end of a promising relationship, Kevin realized the pattern wasn't just bad luck. He started journaling about his feelings after each breakup, discovering a deeper discomfort with trust and vulnerability. With time, his entries formed a map of repeated mistakes.

Kevin spoke honestly about these realizations with his sister, who suggested therapy. With his therapist, Kevin learned that his fears stemmed from past family dynamics. Naming his behavior in this way gave him power. Instead of blaming himself for failed love, he saw actionable steps. He practiced simple, daily acts of trust: letting partners know when he felt anxious rather than retreating, apologizing quickly after arguments, and asking for reassurance when needed. This gradual self-awareness led to stronger, more resilient relationships. He found that sharing his struggle honestly with friends and family created a net of support, encouraging him to keep moving forward.

Relying on Others for Accountability

Support was also a lifeline for Maya, who struggled with binge eating. Maya spent years hiding her eating patterns, swinging from rigid meal plans to secretive binges late at night. The turning point came after she let a close friend in on her secret. There was no judgment, only concern and a gentle suggestion to join a support group. In the group, Maya met others who described her the same feelings and habits. This sense of belonging helped her drop the shame that had always trailed her efforts to change.

With the group's encouragement, Maya adopted small, manageable steps instead of massive, unsustainable overhauls. She texted group members for support, scheduled check-ins, and celebrated little wins, like choosing to call a friend instead of reaching for snacks during an emotional moment. Years later, she describes herself as "in recovery," and while setbacks happen, support keeps her from sliding back into isolation.

Practical Strategies for Change

Building awareness starts with honest reflection, a willingness to see patterns not as fixed traits but as habits with roots and reasons. Journaling after strong reactions, seeking objective viewpoints from trusted people, and even recording short voice notes can make patterns visible. Once the pattern is recognized, change follows small acts of courage—speaking up, reaching out, and practicing self-kindness. Support systems matter. Sharing goals with safe people, seeking mentors, and joining groups make setbacks less daunting.

Celebrating progress is essential, even if the steps are small. Long-term change looks like greater self-compassion, stronger relationships, and a future shaped by choices rather than old fears. Ultimately, the hope these stories offer is simple: anyone can begin, and support makes the journey lighter. Change, while challenging, is not out of reach; it's built from the decision to notice, name, and nurture better habits, one day at a time.

Lessons Learned

Now that we understand how self-sabotage sneaks into our work, relationships, and even struggles with addiction, we can start spotting these patterns in our own lives. Recognizing the ways pride, fear, and old pain hold us back is the first step toward change. With awareness, honest conversations, and a bit of support, it's possible to break free from these cycles and build healthier habits. Recovery and growth don't happen overnight, but every small choice to listen, reach out, or show ourselves kindness moves us closer to the life we really want. The door to lasting change is open—we just have to take that first step through it.

Breaking The Cycle We Built

- Which small decisions or habits in your daily life seem harmless but might be quietly sabotaging your progress?

- Can you identify moments when pride, fear, or old wounds influenced your choices more than logic or intention?

- How does your response to criticism or oversight reveal underlying fears or insecurities?

- What patterns might be holding you back from professional growth, and how can you spot them early?

- How do old wounds or past disappointments influence the way you treat loved ones today?

- How do moments of exhaustion, shame, or guilt influence decisions you later regret?

- What one reflection or insight from this chapter can you act on immediately to begin a positive change?

Chapter Six
The Cost of Ignoring the Warning Signs

"I can't keep doing this," I whispered into the quiet room, staring at the cracked photo frame on my nightstand.

The regrets, the missed calls, the moments I'd chosen to walk away rather than face the pain, they all pressed in like a weight I couldn't shake. Weeks had turned into months, and somewhere along the way, the little alarms inside me, the nudges to ask for help, to make a small change, had grown silent. It felt easier to pretend everything was fine than to deal with what lay beneath. But pretending came with a price, one that wasn't just mine to bear. That night, alone with my thoughts, I finally understood how much ignoring those early warning signs cost me and those I cared about.

Spiritual Drift and Isolation: The Emotional and Spiritual Toll

It can feel like just another rough patch at first. You miss a few mornings of quiet reflection, skip a favorite spiritual ritual, or brush off the urge to reach out for guidance when life gets overwhelming. These moments often pass unnoticed, especially when daily stresses pile up. Yet, when ignored over and over, these warning signs quietly chip away at your spiritual core. You begin to sense a growing distance between your heart and whatever comforted you before. Prayers once spoken with conviction start to feel empty, rituals lose their warmth, and old sources of inspiration run dry. That small voice inside, the one that once guided you, becomes hard to hear.

Repeated self-sabotage wears down spiritual resilience in subtle but powerful ways. For instance, someone might frequently promise themselves to avoid negative habits, only to stumble again. With each attempt and failure, their confidence in personal change erodes. Doubt seeps in, questioning whether lasting transformation is ever possible. This cloud of uncertainty often grows until it blots out faith, leaving a person stranded in confusion. Imagine a woman who used to volunteer at her church every week, finding meaning and belonging in service. She makes a few choices she regrets, feels judged, and sheepishly pulls away. Guilt settles in, whispering that she is no longer worthy. Eventually, she stops attending altogether, missing the comfort that once steadied her through hard times.

When guilt and shame take the wheel, they drive people to further distance themselves from what matters most. Suppose someone finds relief in moments of meditation, but after a string of impulsive decisions, begins to believe they don't belong in that sacred space. The idea of facing themselves, let alone any higher power, feels unbearable. Shame becomes the barrier. Instead of returning to practices that could help heal the wounds, they turn away, deepening the wedge between intention and action. The daily absence of those calming habits leaves a void, gradually filled with regret and bitterness.

This widening spiritual distance does not just stay in the abstract. It often shows up in fractured relationships with friends and family. When shame festers, the natural urge is to conceal mistakes or pain. Consider a man who once confided in his sister when he struggled, but now feels embarrassed about a repeated relapse. Instead of opening up, he avoids her calls, cancels plans, and shrinks from family gatherings. What starts as self-protection feels safer in the short term, but it quickly breeds loneliness.

Isolation rarely happens all at once. It's the friend who stops dropping by, thinking they're only sparing themselves awkward conversations. It's the mother who leaves online messages unanswered because she worries she'll have to explain her setbacks. Gradually, support networks start to thin out. Loved ones sense the withdrawal but feel helpless to break through the wall of silence. Broken trust can linger, too. When someone betrays a friend's confidence by hiding the truth or breaking a promise, it can take years to repair the foundation. Some never build it again. This broken trust casts a long shadow, making it even more difficult to reach out next time, for fear of rejection or judgment.

As distances within relationships grow, loneliness intensifies. People often try to fill that emptiness with quick fixes, more impulsive decisions, or habits that briefly distract, but only deepen the pain afterward. The sense of being cut off sharpens every negative feeling and can drive someone further into cycles of self-doubt and sabotage. Imagine a young adult who, after failing to achieve a goal, turns down invitations and spends weekends alone. Each missed gathering and friendly text left unanswered makes it harder to reconnect, convincing them that others wouldn't understand or forgive. This isolation breeds a heavy sadness that colors even the happiest memories.

Over time, unchecked patterns of self-sabotage and emotional withdrawal can crowd out chances for real growth, forgiveness, and belonging. Life offers countless opportunities for connection, healing, and meaning, but when warning signs are ignored, these moments pass by unnoticed. The cost is felt not only inside the spirit, but within every circle of relationships and missed possibilities, where steps toward healing and authenticity remain just out of reach. The powerful grip of neglecting these signals quietly shapes everything that follows.

Missed Opportunities: Lost Chances for Growth and Fulfillment

There's a particular ache that comes from realizing how much has slipped away because of choices made in moments of fear, doubt, or neglect. Self-sabotage rarely leaves scars on the surface, but its wounds run deep and quiet, often going unnoticed until the evidence—missed opportunities that slowly accumulate—appears. The weight of not listening to those gentle, persistent inner warnings can grow over time, making the air between people denser and the connection with our own sense of purpose more distant.

When isolation takes root, it becomes easy to drift through experiences without true engagement. Consider the story of Anna, who ignored her persistent longing to learn music. She always found reasons to put it off: self-doubt, the belief she was too old, and the fear of failure. She scrolled enviously through others' achievements, convinced she couldn't do the same. In time, the nagging urge subsided, replaced by a dull, hollow regret. She found herself attending concerts, feeling not awe, but a sense of loss. The opportunity to create, to find solace and joy in music, had passed by almost silently. It is not the absence of talent that hurts, but the absence of trying.

The consequences are not limited to personal passions. Relationships suffer as well. James, for instance, carried unspoken apologies for years but never found the courage to reach out to his estranged brother. Each family gathering reminded him of the chasm that had opened between them. A warning sign, the familiar pang of guilt and longing, would flare up, but he always pushed it aside, convincing himself there would be another chance. Years passed, and the brother moved away. By the time James realized how much he missed having a sibling's companionship, the opportunity to reconnect had faded. The cost was not just an unhealed relationship, but the moments and laughter that would never return.

Spiritual drift adds another layer to these losses. Many people experience a call, a gentle nudge toward something greater, a purpose or higher calling, but ignore it in the noise of daily life. Each time the call is set aside, it becomes fainter, easier to dismiss. Eventually, the sense of connection to something larger erodes, leaving only questions and the haunting wonder of what might have been. This spiritual emptiness is often subtle, manifesting as restlessness, a recurring sense that something is missing, yet not knowing what.

Unrecognized self-sabotage can even quietly close doors to meaningful careers or life paths. Imagine someone who dreams of teaching but never applies for the program, always believing someone else is more qualified. Over time, they take jobs they don't care about, watching their passion give way to resignation. The classrooms they might have inspired, the young lives they could have touched, remain only a shadow of what could have been. The loss here is not just personal; it is collective, as countless unnamed students miss the guidance and encouragement only they could have provided.

The Texture of Regret

Regret is a feeling with many shades. For some, it arrives suddenly, sharp and overwhelming. For others, it seeps in gradually, a quiet realization, years after the fact, that an opportunity slipped away because they ignored the signals. It is the longing to rewind time, to seize a chance that is now forever out of reach. These moments haunt people in unexpected ways: seeing a friendship flourish between others and recalling the one that faded, encountering someone living their passion and feeling the ache of unfulfilled dreams. Regret lingers because the missed moments were never truly lost on the world; they simply went unrealized, like seeds that never sprouted.

Why Attention Matters

Self-sabotage is not always dramatic. It can be as simple as saying no to a conversation, leaving a message unsent, or letting self-doubt dictate silence. But repeated often enough, these small acts become a pattern. Ignoring warning signs doesn't just put happiness and fulfillment at risk in the short term; it steadily erodes the landscape of a person's life, making the horizon ever more limited. Over time, the cost is not measured in single moments, but in dreams deferred, relationships that never heal, and a spirit that grows weary of waiting for a chance that never comes.

The effects of missed opportunities extend beyond the individual. When loss becomes a pattern, it shapes how families interact, how children learn to approach risk, and what kind of legacy is left for the next generation. Unspoken pain and unrealized dreams have a way of echoing through families, subtly teaching others to ignore their own warning signs. The quiet consequences ripple outward, shaping futures in ways that are both invisible and profound.

Legacy of Pain: Generational and Long-Term Consequences

Pain that goes unresolved does not simply disappear. It lingers and shapes choices in ways that can be hard to see at first. Over time, these choices add up, touching not only the person who first felt the sting but also everyone close to them. Nowhere is this more true than within a family. The patterns that one person slips into, out of old pain or learned helplessness, quickly become the quiet lessons that children absorb just by living in the same house. Even if no one talks about it, children notice when hope is given up, when dreams are abandoned, or when people stop listening to one another. Children are always watching, and they internalize what is modeled before them. This is how self-sabotage, though it may wear many faces, ends up quietly shaping the lives of the next generation.

Families often build their daily rituals and expectations around invisible rules born from past hurts. If a parent has learned to expect the worst, their doubt may leak out in small sighs, harsh words, or constant warnings. If expressing emotions brought trouble in the past, the family may keep feelings bottled up. Children learn from this. They see that in their family, trusting others is risky, vulnerability is unsafe, and reaching for something better might not be worth it. These are not spoken lessons, but they stick. Over the years, these quiet messages tell children what is normal and what to expect from themselves and the world.

Consider a parent who carries deep-seated shame. Perhaps they fail to step forward in important moments because they doubt their worth, or they apologize for everything, even their own successes. The children in this household notice. Some may become apologetic for existing, thinking they too must shrink themselves. Others may act out, loud and difficult, testing the boundaries set by shame. A different child may chase perfection, desperate to avoid disappointing anyone. In every case, the pain that the parent cannot escape becomes a template for what is possible.

Generational cycles operate in this silence. One generation's unspoken pain sets the script for the next. A mother who avoids conflict because she once got hurt teaches her children to swallow their anger or walk away from hard conversations. A father whose anxiety keeps him from meeting new people passes on the expectation that safety only comes from playing small. It may not be obvious, but children learn the rules of relationship and selfhood from what the adults do, not what they say. When these rules go unchallenged, families become home to patterns that repeat year after year, slowly becoming invisible. In time, no one remembers where the pain started.

The legacy left by self-sabotage touches every part of a child's life. It influences their sense of what is possible in relationships. It shapes how much they trust others or how likely they are to share their feelings. It affects the risks they are willing to take, the dreams they are bold enough to pursue, and whether they believe healing is even possible. Sometimes, it even shapes faith itself. If pain or neglect comes from someone trusted, it can chip away at a child's belief in goodness, trustworthiness, or the hope that things can change.

Simple, daily moments communicate these lessons. The tone of a family meal, the way a secret is handled, the words said about making mistakes, all these become part of a legacy. If apologies are rare, children may not learn how to repair trust. If mistakes bring harsh punishment, they may avoid trying altogether. Even silence teaches powerfully. What is not spoken about, what is always ignored, tells children their pain does not matter.

This cycle can be broken, but it takes more than good intentions. Change begins when someone becomes aware of the legacy they are part of. Counseling can help uncover the old wounds driving today's choices. Honest conversation within a family can let in sunlight where there was once only secrecy. Choosing, every day, to respond differently than before is a powerful act. Instead of hiding shame or repeating old patterns, a parent can show their child what healing looks like by admitting when they need help, by apologizing, and by celebrating small victories.

A new legacy is possible. When one person chooses to heal, it does not end with them. The hope caught by a child's eyes, the warmth in a newly honest family conversation, the decision to comfort rather than judge, it's these small changes that forge a different future. The legacy shifts from pain to hope, and the chain breaks. This is the true power of seeing warning signs and acting before it is too late.

Final Thoughts

Now that we understand how ignoring those inner warning signs and falling into patterns of self-sabotage can quietly harm our spirit, damage relationships, and even shape future generations, we have the power to change course. Paying attention to these signals isn't about blame; it's about caring enough to stop the cycle before it takes more from us and those we love. By facing our struggles with honesty, reaching out for support, and choosing small acts of healing every day, we can rebuild trust, restore connection, and open the door to new opportunities. It won't always be easy, but this journey toward awareness and action offers a chance to rewrite the story for ourselves, our families, and the legacy we leave behind.

Thoughts To Sit With

- When was the last time I felt a nudge to change, reach out, or slow down but chose not to? Why?

- Do I tend to avoid discomfort, conversations, or truths that could actually help me heal?

- In what areas am I quietly convincing myself that "I'm fine," even when I'm not?

- Have guilt, shame, or repeated setbacks made me pull away from my faith or personal grounding practices?

- What spiritual habits or moments of peace have I let slip, and how has that affected my daily life?

- Is there someone I miss but haven't reached out to because of guilt or fear of judgment?

- How might my relationships change if I chose honesty over hiding?

- What is one warning sign I will commit to paying attention to from now on?

- Where in my life can I choose healing instead of hiding?

Chapter Seven
Collateral Damage: How Self-Sabotage Contaminates Relationships

"**N**ina, why won't you just tell me what's on your mind?" Alex asked one evening, his voice soft but tinged with frustration. She shrugged, offering a quick joke instead, and then turned away, leaving the question hanging in the air between them. Moments like this had become their new normal—small silences stretching longer, questions dismissed as if they didn't matter. Neither wanted to admit how scared they were of getting too close, or how that fear was quietly pushing them apart. It wasn't just Nina and Alex; so many of us build walls around the parts of ourselves that feel vulnerable, even when all we really want is to be understood and accepted. But those walls can start to crumble the very connections we need most, between partners, family members, and even coworkers. Sometimes, without realizing it, we're the ones setting the traps that keep love, trust, and success out of reach.

Romantic Partnerships Under Siege

Nina starts shutting down whenever her partner, Alex, gently tries to talk about their future together. She cracks jokes to deflect, dodges sincere questions with sarcasm, and sometimes just leaves the room. For years, Nina's most comfortable armor has been distance. She's terrified of being laughed at for wanting more or, worse, getting rejected for showing her real needs. What she doesn't see is the confusion in Alex's eyes and the growing gap between them. To Alex, Nina's retreat looks like she doesn't care. Trust weakens. The more Nina pulls away for protection, the more Alex feels alone and unappreciated. This tug-of-war in intimacy isn't rare; many people cope with the risk of vulnerability by drawing back, missing out on both genuine closeness and the care they truly crave. What feels like self-preservation slowly masks itself as coldness to the one person who most wants in.

Sabotaging Intimacy

When someone fears vulnerability, the urge to put up barriers becomes overwhelming. It can look like clamming up during conversations, half-listening to a partner's excitement, or making light of moments when real feelings start to surface. These actions aren't about a lack of love; they're protective shields built from old fears and painful memories. Sabotaging intimacy rarely happens in big, obvious gestures. Instead, it's in the small noncommittal replies, the casual cancellations, or pretending to be too tired to talk about anything serious. Partners on the receiving end of these signals often end up feeling undervalued or shut out. Emotional distance, mistaken for disinterest, takes root. Over time, those defenses that once kept someone safe now keep them isolated, longing for comfort while actively pushing it away.

Repeated Arguments

Arguments about the dirty dishes or weekend plans become volcanic because the real fight is buried deep, often in a pit of insecurity. Take Marcus and Jasmine as an example. Marcus grew up doubting his worth, so when Jasmine suggests an improvement or voices a complaint, he hears criticism of his entire character. Fearing exposure of his inadequacies, Marcus lashes out, accusing Jasmine of nagging or picking on him. Instead of asking for reassurance or expressing his worries, he points fingers.

Meanwhile, Jasmine senses his resistance and responds with her own frustrations. Their conversations stop solving problems and start fueling them. The repetition is exhausting, a cycle where neither side feels heard or understood, and the original insecurity remains sealed off and unsaid. Defensive habits like sarcasm, stonewalling, or over-explaining take over. The real feelings—fear of loss, needing validation, craving safety—stay hidden behind the noise of routine fights.

Escalation Checklist:

- Deflecting blame onto a partner

- Criticizing instead of exploring root fears

- Avoiding open, honest talk about what's really wrong

- Letting minor triggers explode into larger battles

Each one sidesteps the cause of tension, so the friction keeps returning, and the emotional climate grows stormier. What seems like unresolved logistics is really an ongoing struggle to feel secure.

Mistrust and Jealousy

Ron came into his relationship with Maya having been betrayed before. Despite Maya's gentle honesty, he reads every delayed reply to a text as a red flag and every new friend as a possible threat. Ron's suspicion isn't rooted in anything Maya's done, but a scar left by a previous partner. He can't help but grill her with probing questions or scroll through her social media when she isn't looking. Over time, Maya feels exhausted and hurt by the constant accusations. Ron's inability to trust casts long shadows; they both start doubting the solidity of their bond. Jealousy like this feeds resentment and underscores every interaction with a feeling of being on trial. The stress of living in anticipation of betrayal chips away at joy and safety. Even well-grounded relationships can be undermined if old wounds are projected onto someone new, setting up a cycle of suspicion and defense that leaves little room for peace.

Avoidance Tactics

When it all feels too much, some people take refuge in busyness. Kelly pours herself into work, volunteering for overtime until her evenings fill up. At home, she scrolls endlessly through her phone, tuning out her partner's questions. She tells herself she's just tired, but beneath the surface is a fear of emotional confrontation. Honest conversations feel risky, so staying busy is more comfortable than facing disappointment or vulnerability. These distractions may prevent immediate discomfort, but they create an ever-widening gulf between partners. Over time, daily avoidance becomes a habit. The emotional connection fades, replaced by a quiet loneliness, even though both people are still sharing a roof.

Patterns like these don't just touch couples. Their echoes ripple into how adults relate within their families, shaping how they communicate with children, model behavior, and build future relationships. The tensions and learned defenses in romantic partnerships often become blueprints for the next generation, gently folding into the fabric of family life.

Family Dynamics and the Parent-Child Cycle

The home is often where vulnerability, fear, and insecurity show up most honestly. People bring their rawest selves to the family table, which sometimes means the habits that protect them in other relationships creep into parenting. Frustration, anxiety, and the worry of not being "enough" color everyday interactions with children. When adults feel unsure about themselves, the urge to maintain order and control can take over. Critical parenting often emerges from this inner landscape of self-doubt. It is not always easy to spot at first. It may look like a parent who points out every little error on a child's homework, fixes each misstep before the child learns on their own, or sets expectations so high that failure feels inevitable. The parent tells themselves they are pushing their child to succeed, but what the child hears is: nothing you do will ever be good enough.

Research shows that children who receive constant criticism or endure rigid perfectionist standards often internalize a sense of unworthiness. According to psychologist Dr. John Gottman, the "emotional coaching" style, where encouragement and acceptance predominate, helps kids develop internal confidence, whereas sharp criticism chips away at that foundation. Over time, kids raised under a cloud of harsh evaluation may develop low self-esteem, doubt their abilities, or become afraid of taking risks. The parents' attempt to protect against failure or rejection accidentally seeds the very insecurity they hope to avoid.

Emotional distance takes root in different ways. Some parents, shaped by hard memories or colder upbringings, pull back without realizing it. A mother, for example, who never felt loved as a child may find it difficult to hug her own kids or say "I'm proud of you." Instead, she may check in about grades or chores, but conversation rarely ventures into feelings. A father who carries wounds from a strict, stoic household may default to short exchanges, steering clear of any talk about sadness or fear. These parents do not mean to create walls. They are often protecting themselves from vulnerability or painful memories.

Children are good at picking up on emotional temperature. They notice when a parent avoids eye contact during important talks or changes the subject when things get personal. Over time, this distance can leave kids feeling unseen or unloved. They may wonder if their feelings matter or if something about them pushes their parent away. Kids who grow up with emotionally distant caregivers may develop trouble forming close bonds, second-guessing whether others will really be there for them. The original intention—to keep uncomfortable feelings at bay—turns into a pattern that affects the next generation.

Destructive cycles slip from one generation to the next in subtle ways. Family stories, unspoken rules, and daily routines all shape what children come to expect from close relationships. If a child grows up hearing criticism instead of encouragement, or watching parents hide problems instead of facing them, those lessons stick. Sometimes, the parent who criticizes was once a criticized child themselves. The emotionally distant parent may have grown up in a home cloaked in silence. Researchers find that self-sabotaging habits, whether criticism, avoidance, or shutting down during conflict, often run in families. Children absorb coping skills from their parents, copying both the strengths and the struggles.

The cycle deepens as family culture normalizes these patterns. Siblings may tease each other in ways that sting, echoing the tone set by parents. Family dinners might be quiet affairs, tension filling up the space where caring words should be. Without realizing it, each generation hands down an instruction manual on how to love and be loved, sometimes full of errors and crossed-out lines.

Some families choose to break this chain and write new chapters. Redemption arcs start with recognition, a parent pausing to notice not only their child's pain, but their own. Real change often begins when parents admit their fear of repeating old patterns or acknowledge mistakes openly. A mother who always corrected her daughter's every move might seek help from a therapist, learning to offer praise and let go of perfection. A father who kept a tough exterior could decide to have honest talks, telling his kids when he feels sad or confused. These moments of openness change the climate at home, making it safer for everyone to be real.

Such families see the benefits ripple outward. Children start to share more, trust grows stronger, and laughter becomes more frequent. Small acts, like apologizing after losing one's temper, writing an encouraging note, or listening without judgment, will add up over time. The work is rarely perfect, but it lays the groundwork for a different legacy, one marked by understanding and resilience.

Echoes of self-sabotage often spill out of family life, touching how adults interact in other settings. These same patterns wait quietly for the moment they will shape new arenas, such as work life, where the stakes and relationships change, but the underlying fears remain familiar.

Sabotage in the Workplace: The Hidden Career Killer

Pushing off important tasks at work often feels harmless in the moment, yet chronic procrastination quietly piles up consequences that reach far beyond a cluttered inbox. Many professionals learn avoidance early, sometimes shaped by childhood fears of criticism or failure, and carry those habits straight into the workplace. The workplace brings its own set of pressures, and when an employee worries that any mistake means they aren't good enough, they may freeze, overthink, or avoid delivering results. Take the manager who says, "I work best under pressure," yet consistently scrambles at the last minute and misses key deliverables. Colleagues start to lose faith, team members stop relying on them, and supervisors rethink future opportunities. In some offices, a single missed deadline can shift a whole project's trajectory, souring clients and eroding trust quickly.

Fear plays a starring role here, specifically, the fear of being judged as not smart, not creative, or not worthy. Employees might set impossible standards, thinking that if their report isn't perfect, it's safest not to submit it at all. Others procrastinate because they secretly believe they're doomed to fail no matter what effort they put in. These patterns, often learned in the family as coping strategies, can zap professional growth. It's easy to see how these fears blend into patterns from home, where perfectionism or criticism once loomed. By becoming more aware of these underlying anxieties, people can start building healthier habits: breaking big tasks into smaller steps, agreeing to incremental deadlines, or asking a trusted colleague to check in for accountability. These small shifts make it easier to act despite fear, rather than being ruled by it.

Another common trap is impostor syndrome, a sneaky belief that all success is accidental and that sooner or later, everyone will realize there's a fraud in their midst. Even the most skilled professionals fall prey to it, regardless of how impressive their work is. Picture the top-performing analyst who, after presenting a widely praised report, quietly tells herself she just "got lucky." Or the team leader who assumes he was only chosen to head a new project because no one else wanted the job. This self-doubt rarely stays contained. Employees gripped by impostor feelings often hold back from voicing strong ideas, hesitate to take on visible assignments, or avoid asking for promotions entirely.

The impact ripples into team dynamics. Colleagues notice the hesitation and reluctance, which may be interpreted as disinterest or lack of leadership. This further leads to missed chances for meaningful collaboration, stalled innovation, or diminished morale across the group. The projects themselves suffer, since the people with vital insight or drive hold back, convinced they don't belong at the table. Learning to name impostor feelings is the first step in loosening their grip. When employees say out loud, "I'm struggling with impostor syndrome," they begin to question whether their doubts are accurate. Small acts like keeping a log of real accomplishments, sharing concerns with a mentor, or simply discussing the feelings at work, can demystify the anxiety and rebuild real self-confidence.

Openness at work isn't always a bad thing, but sharing the wrong information with the wrong person is a classic self-sabotage trap. Some employees, long used to oversharing in family settings, bring this habit to work, unloading personal challenges or emotional struggles in inappropriate settings. Imagine an employee confiding in a new coworker about struggles with burnout, only to have the story circulate through the grapevine. Suddenly, they're seen not for their accomplishments, but for their fraught emotional state. In some organizations, oversharing leads to harmful gossip, professional distance, or even career stagnation.

Yet a real connection is possible through thoughtful disclosure. Healthy vulnerability—like sharing a past work challenge during a trust-building session—can create space for others to open up and foster genuine teamwork. The key is discernment: knowing the difference between a constructive, context-appropriate share and offloading sensitive details indiscriminately. Checking whether a relationship is built on trust, considering the timing, and weighing the relevance of the personal information all help employees keep boundaries in place, making it less likely that openness backfires.

Career advancement brings its own set of risks, and for many professionals, just the thought of a promotion sparks an undercurrent of dread. The fear of higher expectations, increased visibility, or the possibility of public failure pushes some employees to hold themselves back. A skilled team member might quietly pass on a leadership role, telling herself she isn't ready, even when others know she's the best candidate. Others might underperform on purpose, subconsciously hoping to avoid notice and keep the demands of a higher role at bay.

These self-limiting moves often come from old doubts: fear of being outed as incompetent or belief that past mistakes predict future failure. Recognizing this fear and reframing it, like viewing advancement as a chance to grow, not as a public test to be survived, can rekindle ambition. Speaking with mentors, accepting gradual increases in responsibility, or learning from trusted colleagues helps break the cycle. Each step forward sends a powerful message: readiness isn't perfection but willingness to learn and adapt.

Bringing It All Together

Now that we've seen how self-sabotage quietly chips away at our closest relationships, whether with a partner, family, or at work, it's clear these patterns don't have to control us. Understanding where these behaviors come from and how they play out gives us the power to spot them early and choose a different path. By learning to face our fears instead of running from them, we open the door to deeper connections, greater trust, and new opportunities for growth. Change won't happen overnight, but with small steps like honest conversations, setting boundaries, and asking for support, we can break free from old habits and build healthier, more fulfilling relationships in every part of our lives.

Facing the Mirrors You Hide From

- How are you unknowingly putting up walls in your closest relationships, and why do you think you do it?

- How do you respond to vulnerability—your own and others'—and what patterns might be keeping you emotionally distant?

- Are there recurring arguments or misunderstandings in your relationships that reveal your deeper fears or insecurities?

- How might your past experiences or old wounds be shaping the way you trust or mistrust others today?

- Do you notice yourself avoiding difficult conversations or responsibilities at home or at work, and what is driving that avoidance?

- How could your habits—like overworking, over-sharing, or holding back—be affecting the people around you, including family and colleagues?

- What small, intentional steps can you take to break self-sabotaging patterns and build healthier, more authentic connections?

Chapter Eight
Breaking Minds:
The Mental Health Price of Self-Sabotage

We all have moments when our own minds seem to turn against us. The voice inside can be sharp and unforgiving, planting seeds of doubt that grow into barriers we struggle to overcome. These invisible battles affect how we see ourselves and the world, quietly shaping our choices and emotions in ways that are hard to notice but impossible to ignore. Whether it's a nagging feeling of not being good enough or an overwhelming fear of failure, many people fall into familiar patterns that keep them stuck and struggling.

We'll look at how these patterns show up in both modern psychology and ancient stories, revealing truths that cross time and culture. Along the way, practical steps will offer ways to interrupt destructive thinking and build resilience. The goal is simple: to help you recognize these cycles and find new paths toward hope and strength.

The Anatomy of Emotional Turmoil and Its Biblical Reflections

Everyone talks to themselves, but not everyone recognizes the power these inner conversations hold. Negative self-talk, those critical statements repeated inside your head, often operates invisibly. Picture someone late to work for the third time in a month. Almost before the apology, a voice whispers, "I just can't do things right." For others, the refrain might be, "I'm so careless," or "Nobody really wants me around." Over days and weeks, these thoughts become self-declared truths. Eventually, they carve deep tracks of doubt that feel impossible to escape. The mind becomes a loop of reminders about personal shortcomings, quietly eroding confidence and momentum. These scripts may start small, sparked by a harsh word from a parent or a single mistake at school, but left unchecked, they become ingrained barriers. Unmasking these patterns and recognizing how often they echo through daily moments—a missed appointment, an awkward comment at dinner—is the first real step toward rewiring them.

Persistent anxiety stands as another relentless force. Its grip often grows from the seeds of fear—fear of failing, of being rejected, of making the wrong move. Chronic anxiety turns every decision into a potential catastrophe. Consider a writer who spends hours revising the first sentence but deletes everything at the first hint of self-doubt. The fear isn't just about making mistakes; it's about being exposed as "not enough." The mind races with anticipated disasters, projecting a future where every risk ends badly. This loop of worry shapes decisions in subtle but powerful ways. People avoid applying for jobs if they might not get them, decline invitations they're afraid to mess up, or drop projects as soon as they sense difficulty. In time, these protective moves backfire. The more someone dodges challenges, the more powerful their fears become. Anxiety intensifies, and avoidance grows until the very situations that might bring growth are rarely faced. Escaping this cycle requires seeing how often imagined futures block real-world opportunities.

The desire for perfection slips in quietly but can dominate every aspect of life. Perfectionism doesn't just set high standards; it raises the bar so high that even excellence feels like falling short. Think of the new manager, praised by the team yet tortured by the single typo on a memo, or the artist discarding canvas after canvas because none match the vision in their mind. In this mindset, every slip is a failure. The focus shifts from progress to flaw-finding, until self-worth depends on achieving the impossible. The pressure compounds, emotions twist, and self-compassion dries up. Even small mistakes become sources of distress that linger much longer than any actual consequence. This relentless internal critic erodes happiness, making success feel empty and fueling a drive that never lets up. It is only when the roots of these unreachable standards are examined that space for grace and growth can reappear.

Failure and disappointment often trigger a deeper despair. What begins as a single setback, the lost job, the broken promise, the failed relationship, can spiral into a conviction that things will never improve. This despair loop isn't just sadness; it's a lens that makes every future effort seem pointless. Each setback confirms the narrative: "This always happens to me." With each pass through disappointment, the brain grows more certain that hope is foolish, that change is unlikely, and that trying again is a waste. This mindset feeds on itself, driving deeper into helplessness. Over time, these layers of defeat grow thick enough to block out not only motivation but also the belief that new outcomes are possible. Real change begins by seeing the loop for what it is, a distortion, not reality.

Turning to the stories in scripture, the mechanics of these thought patterns come into even sharper focus. Elijah, a prophet worn thin by isolation and fear, collapses in the wilderness after his greatest achievement. Despite witnessing miracles, he flees, overwhelmed by dread and loneliness. He believes he is utterly alone, unworthy, and doomed. His retreat is the ancient echo of anxiety and exhaustion, the sense that victory doesn't chase away uncertainty, and doubts can feel greater than any success. David's psalms capture cycles of regret and self-reproach. Again and again, he mourns his mistakes, questions his worth, and pleads for relief from the guilt that shadows him. These emotions fuel the same loops described above:

disappointment leading to self-judgment, which fosters despair and breeds further self-doubt. Their struggles, written thousands of years ago, mirror the daily struggles faced by so many today.

These patterns lead to a central realization: inner battles shape the course of every life, regardless of era. The stories, whether personal or biblical, illustrate the enduring reality that negative thinking is not unique to any one person or time. Recognizing these patterns can spark the courage needed to seek practical, lasting change and point the way toward more tools and wisdom for breaking the cycle.

Lessons From Suffering: Ancient Stories and Modern Patterns

Everyone struggles with inner forces that seem to turn against us. Negative self-talk, ongoing anxiety, and cycles of despair are common experiences, modern labels for battles that have always taken place beneath the surface. These psychological storms are not new inventions. Ancient stories, such as those of Job and Jeremiah, lay them bare with unforgettable vividness. Their lives remind us that the struggle with self-sabotage is as old as human longing and fear.

The story of Job opens with unimaginable loss. He loses his children, his wealth, his health, and almost all support from those around him. The inner agony that follows becomes an open wound. Job's head spins with unanswerable questions: "Why did this happen?" "What is the point of trying to do right?"

His friends offer hollow answers, but Job refuses to hide his confusion or mask his suffering. At one point, he wails, "My days are swifter than a weaver's shuttle, and they come to an end without hope." His honesty is painful and courageous. Instead of shrinking from his doubts, Job confronts them head-on, even when doing so is exhausting and brings no immediate comfort.

Job's experience shows a mind caught in a loop of defeat and searching. The loss of everything meaningful pushes him into a pit where even self-worth feels out of reach. He wonders aloud if he is being punished, asks what he might have done to deserve his fate, and recoils from the idea that any effort toward goodness matters at all. This spiral, where each question begets another, closely resembles the thinking patterns of modern depression or chronic dissatisfaction. There's no resolve to sugarcoat his pain. For many today, Job becomes a mirror held up to the silent, private doubts that surface on the worst of days. In voicing his despair, Job models a form of honesty that allows for hope to begin—not through forced optimism, but through transparency and the possibility of change.

Jeremiah, called the "weeping prophet," threads a path through a different but equally heavy night of the soul. His words, especially in the book of Lamentations, read like a confession and a cry. He admits to feeling overwhelmed. "My soul is bereft of peace; I have forgotten what happiness is." Adrift in disappointment, Jeremiah describes days when his sense of purpose dissolves into the background noise of hopelessness.

"Why was I ever born?" he moans, giving voice to questions no one wants to admit but many do entertain at the lowest points. Jeremiah's grief does not move in tidy stages, nor does it vanish by force of will. Every setback compounds his pain.

What comes alive in Jeremiah's story is his willingness to lean into vulnerability. Instead of shaming himself for sorrow that will not lift, he brings it to light. He names his sadness, records it, and lets it breathe. In doing so, Jeremiah's anguish opens a quiet door for readers: you are not alone, your despair is not a personal failing, and acknowledging pain does not mean you have lost the fight. Modern struggles with sadness, burnout, or feeling stuck often follow this same shape. They echo Jeremiah's journey—a road marked by grit, days of darkness, and, sometimes, a flicker of hope reigniting when least expected.

Patterns in Job and Jeremiah's emotional lives—ruminating on past losses, questioning their identity, doubting that things will ever improve—are the very patterns seen in contemporary self-sabotage. People today second-guess each decision, replay harsh inner narratives, and slip into chronic defeat. These biblical portraits do more than tell a story; they put language to experiences that are otherwise isolating. Seeing anguish voiced in sacred texts validates emotional suffering and gives it a place at the table.

Reflection can deepen this connection. Personal questions turn wisdom into action: Where do your battles echo Job's confusion? When has Jeremiah's persistent grief echoed your own quiet despair? What would it look like to write out a moment of acute sorrow, or to accept, rather than fight, the length of a sad season? Suggestions such as journaling "Job moments" or identifying with Jeremiah's emotional honesty help chart a course forward. Honesty about weakness is not a dead end. Instead, it softens the ground for gentle change and inner resilience.

By looking honestly at these ancient accounts, a person learns that despair and struggle do not define the soul. Every honest admission of pain can become ground for renewal. With ancient wisdom as a guide and modern strategies for resilience, the suffocating cycles of self-sabotage can be broken. In the places where Job and Jeremiah most struggled, small seeds of transformation start to grow, reminding us that even the deepest nights eventually give way to light.

Interrupting the Cycle: Cognitive-Behavioral and Faith-Based Practices

Thought journaling opens a door to self-awareness, especially when your mind feels tangled by negative thoughts. The point is to grab those hidden beliefs about yourself, things you may not even notice you think, so you can understand and interrupt old, harmful cycles. Job and Jeremiah did not shy away from laying their struggles out, and neither should you. Your pain can be spoken, written, and seen for what it is, rather than being buried.

1. Set aside five minutes each day with a notebook or phone.

2. When a strong emotion hits—like shame, anger, or anxiety—pause and jot down what just happened. Capture what triggered the feeling (a comment from a coworker, a mistake you made).

3. Write out the first thoughts that come to mind without censoring yourself.

4. Later, read your entry and look for patterns. For example, are you telling yourself the same story ("I'm never good enough" or "I always fail") in different situations?

Imagine you got negative feedback at work. Your stomach drops, and by lunchtime, you're convinced everyone thinks you're incapable. You open your journal and write, "Felt stupid and embarrassed. I always let people down." The next time criticism comes, you realize these are familiar thoughts, not facts. Just like Jeremiah named his pain rather than hiding it, putting words to your feelings takes away their power and helps you spot the cycle.

Replacing lies with truth is a way to counteract those painful beliefs that swirl around in your mind. It's hard to believe anything different, especially when hard times seem to confirm your worst fears. But instead of fighting your mind solo, you can anchor yourself in biblical truths—trusting the same promises David held onto while on the run or in despair.

1. Identify a recurring negative belief in your journal (like "I'm worthless" or "I'll always fail").

2. Find a scripture that directly speaks the opposite ("I am fearfully and wonderfully made"—Psalm 139:14, or "I will never leave you nor forsake you"—Deuteronomy 31:6).

3. Write that verse on a card or in your notes app.

4. Memorize it by repeating it aloud three times, morning and night.

5. When negative thoughts show up, say the verse out loud as a direct response.

Picture facing another day where you feel invisible at home or at work. Voices in your head whisper that you don't matter. You remember the scripture you've memorized. As you say, "I am fearfully and wonderfully made," your mind resists at first, but with each repetition, you feel a bit of distance from the old shame. Over time, the truth starts to sound more believable than the lie.

Daily affirmation rituals help you build trust in your worth, one small step at a time. When you pair these affirmations with scripture, you draw on faith and intention together, rewriting the soundtrack of your self-talk before bed and when you get up. It's not about pretending things are perfect. It's about reminding your soul and mind that your story is not finished, and your value is not erased by a hard day.

1. Write or speak a short affirmation each morning, like, "Today, I am loved and supported. I can choose hope over fear."

2. In the evening, reflect for a minute on your day. Pick an affirmation that offers comfort, such as, "Today had challenges. I am still worthy, and I am not alone."

3. As you say or write these words, let yourself notice any emotions—comfort, resistance, even doubt—that rise. Sit with them. Consistency rewrites old scripts.

For example, you finish a long workday and feel like you didn't get enough done. Before sleep, you read your affirmation: "No matter how today ends, I am held by grace. My mistakes do not define me." This nightly act softens the self-judgment. You fall asleep a little lighter, with more hope for tomorrow.

Listing blessings steers your mind from constant self-criticism toward appreciation. David's psalms overflowed with gratitude even in the valleys, and Jeremiah's laments always circled back to hope. Gratitude practice is your way to train your brain, no matter how hard the day is.

1. Each morning or night, list three things you are grateful for (small or big).

2. If the day feels dark, focus on ordinary things—the warmth of coffee, a text from a friend, the sun outside your window.

3. Write them down, say them aloud, or pray about them.

You wake up anxious, already dreading what's ahead. Still, you scribble, "I woke up, I had a filling breakfast, my friend checked in on me." The list seems simple, but you notice a subtle shift—your mood eases. This act, repeated faithfully, builds resilience and replaces scarcity with hope.

When these exercises become habits, emotional storms quiet. You become the author of your own story, not a victim of old voices. These steps, rooted in modern psychology and spiritual truth, give you the power to break sabotaging mental habits. Stay with them, not because change comes fast, but because it comes from showing up for yourself every day.

Bringing It All Together

Now that we understand how self-sabotage takes hold through negative thoughts, anxiety, and perfectionism, echoed even in ancient stories, we have the tools to fight back. Recognizing these patterns is just the start; by practicing honest reflection, leaning on faith, and using simple habits like journaling, affirmations, and gratitude, we can break free from the cycles that hold us down. It won't always be easy or quick, but every small step rewrites the story in our minds. Moving forward, you can take control of your inner voice and build a stronger, kinder relationship with yourself, opening the door to true resilience and hope for what's next.

Listening to the Voices You Ignore

- How are the voices in your mind shaping the way you see yourself and your choices?

- When have you noticed yourself repeating negative self-talk, and how did it affect your actions or mood?

- In what areas of your life do fear and anxiety hold you back from taking risks or pursuing opportunities?

- How does your desire for perfection stop you from celebrating progress or feeling satisfied with your efforts?

- When faced with failure or disappointment, how do you usually respond, and does it create a cycle of self-doubt?

- Which biblical or personal stories of struggle and resilience can you relate to, and what can they teach you about your own challenges?

- What small daily habits—like journaling, affirmations, or gratitude—can you start practicing to interrupt self-sabotaging thoughts and build resilience?

Chapter Nine
Anxiety, Stress, and Depression: The Fruits of Self-Inflicted Pain

Anxiety, stress, and depression aren't just random struggles that happen to us; they often grow from the very ways we handle pressure and doubt. It might feel like these feelings come out of nowhere, but when you take a closer look, they're actually the product of patterns we create ourselves. From the quiet moments spent rehashing mistakes to the times we avoid facing tough situations, these habits quietly chip away at our peace and hope. What's more, for those trying to live out their faith, these inner battles can bring a confusing clash between belief and pain, making it hard to know where to turn. This chapter peels back the layers on how the choices we make in response to fear and worry can deepen the weight on our hearts, and how understanding this can open the door to real healing.

Tracing the Path from Doubt to Disorder: Understanding the Psychological Descent

Everyone seems to know what it feels like when thoughts start looping late at night, and every worry grows louder in the silence. Rumination works its way into the mind, replaying mistakes, forecasting catastrophe, and chewing on what-ifs until exhaustion sets in. Someone who has just finished a challenging meeting at work might catch themselves replaying every word they said, worrying that each one sounded foolish or weak. Instead of resolving concerns and finding answers, they relive embarrassment so often that it begins to feel permanent. Each trip through the mental maze leaves the person feeling smaller, less capable, and more anxious about the next time. Even daily moments like sending an email or deciding whether to join a gathering become opportunities for second-guessing. When these patterns take root, hope gets sapped away. It starts to look impossible to fix things or to imagine a future that feels safe or bright. There's a trap here, built by the mind's habit of feeding on its own unease. These rehearsals rarely lead to creative solutions; instead, they fuel the idea that the worst is bound to happen.

A mind weighed down by constant worry often tries to find relief by stepping away from challenges. Avoidance feels like a handy fix when anxiety climbs too high. Leaving emails unread, canceling plans, or ignoring that awkward conversation gives a momentary shield from discomfort. For example, someone might leave a phone call unreturned, afraid the conversation will be tense or confrontational. The day feels lighter for a while, but some part of the mind lingers in dread. Like weeds, unspoken fears and unresolved tasks multiply. Avoidance teaches the brain that facing uncertainty should be feared, so the next uncomfortable experience seems even bigger and more frightening. Opportunities for growth start to disappear. Invitations go unanswered, new projects are skipped, and relationships drift. Life narrows, choices shrink, and self-confidence weakens. Every time a situation gets dodged, the mind learns a little more to distrust the world and its own ability to handle tough moments. Stress inches up, running like a current beneath everything.

After a while, the body begins to register the toll. An anxious week can bring on pounding headaches that will not go away, even after rest. A tough month might leave someone with a stomach clenched tight enough to ruin their appetite. Nights fill with restless sleep, mornings arrive with a chest weighed down by dread. Sometimes the skin breaks out, the jaw grinds tight, or the pulse climbs just from opening an inbox. These are not imaginary ailments or simple nerves; they are physical signals that the emotional load is too heavy. The body responds to distress as if real danger is present, sending up alarm flares that cannot be ignored or "thought away." Each ache and complaint deepens the sense that things are not right, stoking anxiety about health and well-being. When this cycle takes hold, the brain and body start working in a feedback loop—pain increases tension, tension worsens symptoms, and around it goes.

When mental and physical exhaustion build up together, it robs even the smallest motivations. Tasks that once gave satisfaction or joy seem pointless. Someone who enjoys cooking might start skipping meals, eaten up by worry, or may be too tired to care. The braver moments, like signing up for a class or reconnecting with old friends, feel impossible. Instead of setting goals or making plans, a person might lose entire afternoons scrolling mindlessly or staring out the window, overwhelmed by indecision. The sense of being weighed down leads to checking out, letting chores pile up, and letting friendships fade. The longer these days stretch on, the darker life feels. Purpose slips away, replaced by a heavy fog of hopelessness. This is the point where ongoing anxiety and chronic stress begin to take on the colors of depression. Not even wanting to try becomes a habit of its own, turning setbacks into proof that things will never change. It becomes easier to believe every self-criticism is true.

All these steep drops in well-being grow from patterns that started small: one or two negative thoughts, a skipped event, a missed meal. The pathway to depression, paved with the stones of worry and avoidance, is walked step by step, often in quiet isolation. Yet, the details of personal struggle and hard-won moments of change are as complex and individual as each person affected. There is room in this story for understanding, connection, and tools that bring hope, no matter how subtle or slow they may appear.

Real Stories: When Faith Collides with Fear

A midweek church gathering filled with prayer and praise can hide what's really going on beneath the surface. Among the joyful singing and scripture readings, many believers sit in silence, wrestling with thoughts they dare not speak aloud. Take Sarah, a youth leader, who found herself caught in a relentless loop of rumination. She constantly questioned if her struggles with anxiety meant her faith was weak. Early on, Sarah's negative self-talk drowned out any words of encouragement she heard on Sundays. She kept up her serving, always smiling, but privately journaled every regret, worried that even those closest to her would question her devotion if they discovered her pain. She admitted in a rare conversation, "If I'm supposed to have the peace of Christ, why can't I feel it?" It wasn't just anxiety. The church's casual remark, "Just pray about it," felt like a stamp telling her not to ask deeper questions. So she pressed everything down, her real prayers turning into silent suffering.

Silent Suffering: The Weight of Stigma

This kind of isolation is not unusual. Stories gathered from adults in different churches reveal a pattern. James, a choir member, explained how he went months without anyone noticing his withdrawal. He described arriving late, sitting at the back, and leaving quickly after the service. He worried that admitting to depression would bring judgment or even lose him his ministry position. Instead of voicing his needs, he silently endured, hoping the ache would pass. Others in his congregation confessed to similar experiences, feeling they had to "put on a brave face" or risk being seen as spiritually immature.

The stigma around mental health in many faith settings runs deep, causing people to mask their struggles. Some recall requests for prayer that stayed vague to protect their image. Anna, who had battled panic attacks, once asked her church group for "guidance" rather than confessing her true fears. She worried scripture would be used as a weapon instead of a comfort. This secrecy only led to deeper isolation. More than one person described the emotional toll of pretending, which made recovery even harder. The sense of being misunderstood or dismissed chipped away at their sense of belonging, sometimes pushing them further from the church community they needed most.

Prayer in the Dark: Faith Under Pressure

Yet, in the midst of darkness, faith often becomes both a question and a lifeline. For Chris, despair roared loudest late at night, when sleep stayed out of reach. Alone in his room, he whispered broken prayers, simple, desperate words: "God, help. Please meet me here." He didn't always feel heard, but clung to the habit anyway. Over time, these prayers became a rhythm, less about begging for relief and more about holding onto hope. Chris describes moments where, through his exhaustion, he sensed a subtle steadiness—a thread connecting him to something bigger than his pain.

These stories repeat a theme: believers praying precisely because they cannot see a way forward. Maria, a teacher, wrote prayers in her journal during depressive episodes she called her "gray seasons." She found no instant rescue, but continued to pour out her sorrow. For her, the act of praying itself acknowledged the reality of the pain and the hope it could someday shift.

Spiritual Community Gaps

Many also faced a different kind of hurt, missteps by church leaders or friends that deepened wounds. While some offered gentle support, others replied to confessions of struggle with biblical clichés: "Just have more faith," "God won't give you more than you can handle," or "Rejoice always." For people like Brian, who reached out after months of battling intrusive thoughts, these responses stung. He felt dismissed and ashamed. One woman recalled finally sharing her anxiety with a trusted elder, only to be advised to "pray harder," leaving her feeling more alone than before.

Such well-meaning but shallow responses failed to meet people where they were. They reinforced the idea that mental health struggles are simply a lack of spiritual discipline. This approach often discouraged future honesty, pushing people to either suffer alone or leave in search of understanding.

Moments of Breakthrough

Yet hope broke through in unexpected ways. Some found solace in a genuine friend who simply listened without trying to fix things. For Ben, renewal came during a worship night when he suddenly felt God's nearness amid his pain. He described it not as a cure, but a turning point, a reason to try again. Others pointed to breakthroughs in therapy, where a counselor who shared their values helped blend faith and psychological tools. Faith communities that started mental health groups created safe spaces for honest conversation, giving rise to real connection.

In each case, the shift from silent suffering to hope began with vulnerability and compassionate acceptance. These moments marked the beginning of restoration, a reminder that faith and mental health can exist together, shaping a journey toward healing.

Tools for Restoration: A Christian Approach to Healing

Some days feel heavy with sorrow, confusion, and a longing for healing. During these moments, faith-based approaches can shape the journey toward recovery, offering both practical and spiritual resources for those facing anxiety, stress, or depression. One of the most honest acts involves lament. This means expressing grief, pain, or even anger openly before God. Lament does not close the door to faith; rather, it is proof of an active relationship, a willingness to voice trouble instead of hiding it. Imagine writing in a journal late at night, pouring out disappointment and questions on the pages. As tears come, there is no need to censor the pain. Next, perhaps, a favorite worship song plays quietly from a playlist. As the melody rises, something shifts. The act of singing becomes a reminder that hope and trust still have a place. In this way, lament creates space for honesty, while worship offers a way to anchor attention on God's faithfulness. This dance between acknowledging pain and declaring hope brings balance. It helps the heart let in both truth and trust, making burdens easier to carry.

Often, it is assumed that faith alone should be enough to overcome emotional struggles. This idea can create shame or reluctance to reach for professional help. Yet, just as we would see a doctor for a broken bone, it is wise and courageous to seek therapy or medication when facing mental distress. Far from being a sign of defeat, reaching out honors the body and mind God has given. Therapists, counselors, or psychiatrists use research-backed methods to untangle complex emotions and guide clients toward resilience. For some, medication restores balance in brain chemistry, making it easier to participate in life and relationships. Think of someone named Michael, who, after weeks of sleepless nights and constant worry, finally makes an appointment with a therapist. Over several sessions, Michael discovers that his anxiety's root is a mix of old wounds and pressures from work. When his therapist suggests medication, he hesitates, worrying it reflects doubt or failure. But with time, support, and prayer, Michael sees that relief from overwhelming anxiety is a gift. His ability to sleep improves, making it possible to enjoy quiet mornings with family and breathe easier. Wise stewardship of mental health includes making use of all the tools God places within reach, including qualified help and medical advances.

Scripture serves as another practical anchor during distress. Memorizing specific verses can become a lifeline when panic or hopelessness threatens to take over. In moments when negative thoughts swirl, reciting a verse like "Peace I leave with you; my peace I give you" shifts mental focus and interrupts the flood. Someone might place sticky notes with scripture on their bathroom mirror or set phone reminders with short prayers during the day. Partnering with a friend for accountability, trading encouraging texts with favorite verses, doubles both support and hope. These simple habits provide steady reminders of God's presence and promises, supporting the mind through challenging times.

Physical habits also link closely with emotional healing. Regular movement, even if small, helps clear mental fog and lifts exhaustion. For someone feeling unmotivated, a brisk walk around the neighborhood or gentle stretches in the living room are meaningful first steps. Exercise causes the brain to release endorphins, natural chemicals that boost mood and reduce feelings of pain. Rest is just as important as movement. Creating a bedtime routine such as dimming lights, reading before sleep, or avoiding screens, encourages deeper, more restful sleep. Nutrition, often overlooked, feeds resilience. Simple meals with vegetables, whole grains, and lean protein help balance blood sugar and support focus. Swapping out sugary snacks for a handful of nuts or fruit may stave off energy slumps later in the day. These daily choices increase mental clarity, patience, and positive feelings, making it easier to manage big emotions and stressful situations.

No single practice by itself makes suffering disappear. Instead, honest lament, heartfelt worship, professional care, scripture engagement, and physical self-care work together, covering spiritual and practical needs. Each person's blend will look different, shaped by individual stories and circumstances. Recovery asks for commitment, courage, and grace to try again on hard days. It also invites kindness for yourself as you discover what brings relief. In all these efforts, real transformation grows through repeated, small choices, rooted in the belief that healing is possible and hope is never far away.

Final Thoughts

Now that we understand how our own thoughts and actions can deepen anxiety, stress, and depression, especially when faith feels tangled in the struggle, we can take steps toward healing with both heart and mind. Recognizing the patterns of doubt and avoidance is the first move in breaking free from silence and shame. By embracing honest prayer, seeking support, leaning on scripture, and caring for our bodies, we build a foundation where hope can take root again. Healing doesn't happen overnight, but each small choice to face the hard days with courage and grace brings us closer to restoration. Together, faith and practical tools create a path forward where recovery and peace are truly within reach.

Prompts to Lift the Weight Within

- How do you notice your own thoughts and habits contributing to feelings of anxiety, stress, or depression?

- When have you caught yourself avoiding situations or tasks out of fear, and how did that affect your sense of peace or confidence?

- Are there moments when your faith feels at odds with your emotional struggles? How have you responded to that tension?

- How has stigma—whether from others or yourself—kept you from seeking support or speaking about your mental health?

- What small, daily practices (like journaling, prayer, or scripture memorization) could help you manage overwhelming thoughts and emotions?

- How could combining spiritual habits with professional help—therapy, medication, or counseling—support your overall well-being?

- Which physical or lifestyle habits (sleep, exercise, nutrition) could you adjust to strengthen both your body and mind during stressful periods?

Chapter Ten
Breakthrough Strategies to
Overcome Self-Sabotage

Most of us think self-sabotage is just a matter of willpower or bad habits, but what if the real problem runs much deeper? What if the way we try to fix ourselves is actually making things worse? Breaking free from that cycle isn't about beating yourself up harder or pretending everything's fine. Instead, it's about learning new ways to face your struggles honestly, lean on others, and build simple daily routines that help you heal from the inside out. This chapter dives into fresh strategies that mix heartfelt faith with proven psychological tools—showing you how small steps toward truth and connection can create lasting change when nothing else seems to work.

Modeling Victory: Lessons from the Redeemed

Peter once found himself facing the darkest moment of his life, captured in John 21. After denying Jesus, something he swore he would never do, he was left with shame and regret. He did not try to hide or cover up his mistake. Peter owned up to it fully. When Jesus gave him the chance to speak honestly, Peter did not offer excuses or blame others. He admitted his failure, making space for true forgiveness. Instead of running away, he spoke the truth, showing humility that became the first step in his restoration. By asking Peter again and again, "Do you love me?" Jesus led him through a painful but honest review of his fall. Peter discovered that facing hard truths about himself did not end his story; it started a whole new chapter. He found that humility is not weakness. Rather, it opens the door to growth no matter how deep the shame. Repentance did not shrink Peter or destroy his future. It released him from his past, proving that failures are not final defeats but invitations to real change. When Peter allowed himself to feel regret but refused to stay there, he began to heal. His willingness to say "Yes, I failed" became the turning point, a living lesson in how falling down can lead to a fresh beginning.

Modern stories echo these same life-changing ideas. Take the case of Monica, who struggled for years with destructive workplace habits. She regularly missed deadlines and then spiraled into self-criticism, feeling that she was not good enough to try for anything better. Instead of staying stuck, she made a list of her mistakes like Peter and talked with a trusted friend about her fear of letting people down. With some coaching, Monica learned to break big projects into smaller steps and check in with her supervisor more often. When she started meeting small goals, she wrote them down and celebrated each win, no matter how tiny. Her story proves that perseverance thrives best when paired with tangible, bite-sized actions. Faith in herself grew as she kept promises to herself, flipping the old story in her head about failure being permanent.

Carlos faced a battle against substance abuse, one that made him doubt his self-worth and sabotage his relationships. He tried to handle things alone at first, convinced that no one would understand his struggle. This wall of isolation made setbacks harder. He realized later, after several stumbles, that open conversations with a mentor from his faith community changed the direction of his life. The mentor did not judge but listened, helped Carlos uncover patterns, and encouraged small improvements. Carlos started attending support meetings, writing about his progress in a journal, and practicing daily reflection. The combination of honesty, repeated effort, and consistent checking in made a breakthrough possible. His journey showed that the right help can unlock places inside us where hope has faded.

The Power of Having People in Your Corner

Trusted mentors and accountability partners bring lasting progress that seems out of reach into your hands. Spiritual leaders and personal mentors offer something more powerful than quick fixes: they provide perspective when you feel blinded by disappointment and someone to walk beside you whenever you might slip. These relationships transform isolation into connection and replace shame with honest progress. Mentors do not simply offer advice; they ask hard questions, notice patterns you may have missed, and keep you pointed toward your values, whether or not you feel motivated in the moment. For Monica, inviting her supervisor and friend into her self-improvement plan was the bridge between intention and action. Carlos found that his faith mentor's encouragement kept him focused during tough weeks. Accountability is not about control; it's a source of strength that makes lasting change feel possible.

Real-Life Habits That Anchor Growth

Momentum comes from small, daily habits that anchor progress. Many find that starting their day with prayer, meditation, or a simple gratitude list steers their minds away from old negative loops. Practices such as noting even the smallest victory create a pathway from where you are to where you hope to be. When setbacks come, responding with self-compassion rather than harsh judgment feeds resilience. Others keep a log of daily choices, checking off what went well and admitting what did not. This honest routine does not just measure progress, it teaches patience and builds hope for the next step. Faithful follow-through multiplies results over time. Simple choices like reaching out instead of retreating or reflecting before reacting are the foundation for all the strategies that follow in this chapter. Each habit is a building block, setting up a life where transformation becomes more than wishful thinking.

Practical Battle Plans: Tools for Lasting Change

When you read about Peter's fresh start and heard those stories of ordinary people breaking old habits with the help of friends and faith, it probably felt like a door was opening. You might have sensed that true change isn't out of reach, it's already in motion the moment you say, "Maybe I really could be free of this." Now it's time to move your hope out of your head and into your hands, because the most powerful encouragement often asks us to respond. You're not alone; you've been given practical tools to keep walking, even when it feels hard.

Confession and repentance, for example, are much more than guilt trips. Instead, think of confession as shining a flashlight into a dark corner. It's facing the truth of your choices, not to shame yourself, but to let air and light clean out whatever's been festering. When you sit quietly, take a deep breath, and let your heart name what went wrong, you release some of that secret pressure that keeps you stuck. Repentance is the next step: it's a turn. Not a dramatic, once-in-a-lifetime about-face, but a series of small, honest course corrections that begin with you saying, "I want to move in a better direction." Here's a way to try this. Settle somewhere you feel safe, maybe in your parked car before walking into work, or just before bed. Say out loud or write in a notebook, "God, I'm struggling with..." Name the behavior or thought with clear words. Don't edit yourself. Ask honestly, "Is this how I want to live?" Listen quietly for a moment. Then, picture taking one step away from that behavior, just one concrete thing you could do differently tomorrow. For example, admit to yourself, "I keep picking fights when I'm tired." Decide tonight, "Tomorrow, when I feel irritable after work, I'll take five minutes alone instead of starting an argument." Even this tiny act is repentance. The more often you practice, the lighter you'll feel, and the easier it will become to be honest next time.

Now lean into prayer, but not the kind that sounds stiff. Mindfulness prayer lets you notice your feelings without judging or hiding them. It creates room for God to meet you exactly where you are. Start by setting your phone timer for five minutes. Sit comfortably, close your eyes, and breathe slowly. Silently say, "God, help me notice what's happening inside me right now." Let thoughts and feelings float up. You don't need to solve them or push them away; just name what's there: "I feel angry. I'm worried. I'm tired." After a few breaths, say, "God, thank you for being with me in this. Show me what I need to see." Trust that you're not alone. A real-life example: at lunch, you step away from your desk, close your eyes, and simply notice your racing mind and tense shoulders. You breathe out your frustrations, whisper an honest prayer, and let yourself rest in God's steady presence. Even if worries don't disappear, you return to your tasks with more peace and less urge to self-sabotage.

You don't have to get stuck just thinking and feeling, though. Behavioral activation invites you to act your way out of the rut, even when you're not feeling strong yet. Pick one easy, healthy task you can finish, something that interrupts your usual pattern. Maybe that means texting a friend "I need some encouragement today," clearing your kitchen counter, or standing in the sun for five minutes before your next meeting. The point isn't to overhaul your life, but to prove to yourself that you have the power to do the next right thing. For someone overwhelmed by procrastination, write down just one dreaded phone call you'll make in the morning. Do it, then cross it off. Celebrate that momentum, and let it nudge you forward. These small wins build the muscle of resilience, especially when stacked up day after day.

Personal boundaries make all of this possible. Without them, your best intentions are just words. Boundaries protect your time, your rest; they are fences for your soul. Try this simple script: "I can't take that on right now," or "I want to help, but I need to say no so I can focus on my priorities." Picture yourself on a busy morning, and a coworker asks you to fix a problem that isn't really yours. Instead of jumping in and fueling your frustration, you calmly reply, "I'm sorry, I can't handle that today." Boundaries are acts of both courage and kindness, toward yourself and others.

As these tools come together, you start to see how moments of honesty open space for prayer. Prayer clears a path for meaningful action, and action becomes sustainable when you protect what matters most. Each one supports the other, pushing you forward. The next part of your journey builds on this foundation, helping you turn these new steps into steady rhythms, so freedom gets woven into your regular days. For now, let these practical battle plans carry you forward as you step toward the life you've been hoping for.

Daily Renewal: Building Routines That Heal

Starting each morning with intention builds a foundation for the day. Deliberate acts of devotion disrupt negative self-patterns and root the mind in gratitude and hope. Someone who tends to wake up already dreading the day or fearing they'll fall into old traps can benefit from a devotional routine. It resets mental habits and reconnects with God's acceptance. Mornings shape attitude, and the first thoughts influence self-perception and daily choices. Centering on scripture, prayer, and gratitude can gradually weaken the pull of self-sabotage.

Morning Devotions

1. Before picking up your phone or opening your calendar, settle quietly and speak a simple prayer: "God, thank you for this day. Help me walk in Your love and wisdom."

2. Choose a piece of scripture to anchor you. For extra impact, pick one that speaks against shame or self-criticism, like Romans 8:1: "There is now no condemnation for those who are in Christ Jesus." Say it out loud. Allow the words to settle in your heart before you move on.

3. Write down one thing you're thankful for. It could be as small as a good cup of coffee or as big as family or a safe home. This focuses your mind away from anxiety and sets up a stance of grateful expectation.

4. End with a brief note to yourself: "One way I'll honor myself and God today is…" Then finish the sentence, for example, "…by giving myself grace if I make a mistake, or by asking for help if I feel overwhelmed."

A person who usually starts the day rushed and already criticizing herself might notice over time she is softer with her own missteps after using this method daily. The power lies in returning to these steps every morning, letting the truth of who you are in Christ become the voice that leads you.

Evening Reflections

At night, honest reflection offers closure and a way to process progress without getting stuck in regret. By reviewing actions and realigning with God's acceptance, you can end each day with renewed hope. This breaks the cycle where failure at one point leads to self-sabotage the next day. Evening routines shift focus toward learning and mercy.

- Find a quiet space before bed. Breathe deeply and ask, "God, show me where I lived out your love today."

- Answer reflection questions in a journal or notebook:

  1. What choice am I proud of today?

  2. Where did I sense God's strength helping me?

  3. Did I fall back into old patterns? If so, what might help tomorrow?

  4. What do I want to leave in God's hands tonight?

- If something went wrong, confess it simply: "Jesus, I slipped here, but I trust you to keep growing me." No shame, just honesty.

- Write or pray a thank-you for something small that brought comfort or joy, even in a hard day, maybe a friend's text, a peaceful walk, or simply making it through.

- Close by intentionally letting go of anxieties, even whispering, "God, I trust you as I sleep."

A man working to overcome procrastination might record how he finished a task he dreaded, thank God for energy, and note where he struggled to set boundaries with coworkers. Over time, evenings shift from anxious rumination to peaceful closure.

Weekly Rest

Sustained change won't stick without regular rest. A Sabbath day or another dedicated rest period nourishes the soul and interrupts cycles of striving that drive self-sabotage. Planning rest creates space to enjoy God, relationships, and playfulness, refilling emotional tanks so that self-destructive urges quiet down.

1. Pick one recurring day or half-day each week and block it as untouchable in your schedule.

2. Prepare ahead so major chores or errands are finished before your rest window.

3. During rest time:

    - Turn off email, work notifications, and all non-essential screens.

    - Spend extra time in prayer or scripture, perhaps reading a Psalm or taking a nature walk.

    - Share a meal with others or call a friend; laughter and togetherness are restorative.

    - Do something creative or restful: read, listen to music, nap, or simply linger in the moment.

    - Avoid stressful tasks, planning, or self-criticism—pretend for these hours that striving isn't allowed. If needed, explain your rest boundary to family or colleagues.

Someone who always feels guilty for slowing down may notice guilt ease as rest becomes routine. The world keeps turning, and you discover that your value doesn't depend on constant achievement.

Celebrating Wins

Documenting small victories cements progress and replaces defeat with hope. Recognizing and sharing these wins counters perfectionism and triggers motivation to continue. No win is too small: every step forward deserves acknowledgment.

- After any noticeable moment of growth, pause and jot it down. For example, passing up an old temptation, speaking kindly to yourself, finishing a task early, or reaching out for support.

- Once a week, read through your list of wins. Thank God for his help. Note even the tiny "I set a boundary" or "I got out of bed without dread."

- Share a few wins with an accountability friend or group. A simple text, "I stuck to my morning routine three days this week!" builds support and lets others celebrate with you.

- Pray or reflect after sharing: "God, help me see your hand in each of these moments and keep taking the next right step."

Through marking and celebrating these breakthroughs, the path out of self-sabotage feels less lonely and more hopeful, fueled by the visible fruit of each faithful habit.

Concluding Thoughts

Now that you've seen how honest reflection, faith-filled action, and steady habits can break the cycle of self-sabotage, it's time to take these tools and make them your own. Remember, change doesn't happen all at once. It grows through small, daily steps taken with courage and kindness toward yourself. Lean on trusted friends or mentors when the road feels tough, and let your routines of prayer, reflection, and celebration anchor you in hope. With each moment of truth and every choice to move forward, you're not just surviving, you're stepping into a new story where healing and growth are real and lasting. This chapter has given you a practical blueprint; now it's yours to put into action and watch your life transform day by day.

Unshedding Self-Sabotage with Grace

- What is one act that I resort to that is self-sabotaging but seems like a cure or a fix to my problems? What words will describe that act the most?

- What kind of temporary relief does it provide me, and what might the consequences be if I don't follow through with that particular act?

- What is my usual go-to response? Shame or a corrective or progressive action?

- Who are the people who can be my "anchors" (people I can count on to give me good guidance and motivate me)?

- What is the smallest habit that I can adopt easily to counter my self-sabotaging behavior, something that wouldn't have an exhausting mental or physical toll?

- Whenever I am overwhelmed, what quick and manageable steps or actions can I take to stop me from leaning towards my self-sabotaging behaviors?

- What are the places that demand a strict boundary that I need to enforce as quickly as I can?

- What recent victories have I neglected and failed to celebrate that could have given the due encouragement that I need to bring about a big change?

Chapter Eleven
Freedom's Foundation: Accepting Your Story and Transforming Your Identity

"I can't believe I let that happen again," I whispered to myself, staring at the cracked photo on my shelf.

That moment felt like a weight I carried everywhere, the mistake, the regret, the endless replay in my mind. For years, it shaped how I saw myself, as if my worth was tied only to failures I couldn't erase. But one day, something shifted. I realized that holding onto all that pain wasn't protecting me; it was keeping me stuck. What if I could face my story differently, not by pretending it never happened, but by accepting it with kindness and truth? That quiet thought opened a door I didn't even know was there, a chance to rewrite not what happened but how I lived with it. Sometimes, change begins with just that small step of embracing where you've been, even if it's messy, and learning to see yourself through new eyes.

The Power of Acceptance: Owning Your True Story

Regret often feels like a loop you can't shut off. Maybe it's the sting of an argument with a loved one that pops into your mind every time you see their face, or a career misstep that keeps echoing in decisions years later. It's easy to let these memories define who you are, to let shame build brick by brick until it feels like you're walled off from your own story. But there's a gentle but radical alternative: self-acceptance grounded in grace, not guilt. This looks like facing the pages of your past openly, recognizing that each chapter, even the messy ones, can serve as ground for personal growth and spiritual maturity.

Picture yourself looking back on a moment of failure, the sort that usually leaves your stomach in knots. Instead of rehearsing harsh judgments, try on a new script: "Yes, I made a mistake, but it taught me what not to do and how to say sorry to others, and to myself." For example, Jen, who used to beat herself up every time she remembered an old friendship she let slip away, paused and reminded herself of what that loss taught her. Now, she values honesty in relationships and checks in more thoughtfully with her friends. When regrets become teachers instead of tormentors, the story changes.

A shift like this starts with separating your identity from your choices. You are not your worst moments. One practical way to make this real is by writing a compassionate letter to your younger self. Begin with "Dear me at age ____, I know you were doing the best you could." List what that younger you struggled with, naming both the choices and the fears underneath them. As you write, add words of comfort or even a blessing, the way you'd speak to a dear friend. The goal isn't to sugar-coat, but to acknowledge pain as part of your history, not your identity.

Sometimes regret isn't about a single decision but goes all the way back to childhood wounds, moments when you didn't feel seen, or times when others' mistakes cast long shadows over your confidence. Carrying those hurts can feel like lugging an invisible weight. But what if those very hurts can open the door to deeper empathy? If you grew up with a critical parent, for example, that pain can help you become a more affirming friend or partner. Instead of seeing old wounds as lifelong sentences, use them as catalysts for growth. You gain freedom to respond with grace, to yourself and to others.

Self-compassion doesn't mean excusing everything or avoiding responsibility. It means you treat yourself as someone worthy of care, even in moments you wish you could erase. Pulling from spiritual truth, the promise found in Romans 8:1—"There is now no condemnation for those who are in Christ," can act like an anchor holding you steady, no matter how strong the inner storm gets. Imagine God's love as the unmovable post in the middle of a hurricane, refusing to budge even when regret rages around you. Divine love marks your worth, not the opinions of others or the tally of your past.

Self-Compassion Practices You Can Use

- **Writing a Self-Kindness Message**

Explanation of method: Each morning, grab your journal or even a sticky note. Write one short encouragement to yourself, as if a wise friend were writing it. For example, "You're allowed to start again," or "You handled yesterday's challenge with more courage than you realize."

Sample script: Imagine waking up after a tough day and writing, "Today, I choose to treat myself with patience no matter what comes." Place that message where you'll see it often.

- **Thoughtful Journaling for Regret**

Detailed steps for the method:

1. Recall a memory that usually triggers regret.

2. List the facts, no judgments, just what happened.

3. Write down what you wish you'd done differently.

4. Finish by noting what the experience taught you or how it grew your compassion for others.

Realistic scenario: After reliving a harsh comment made in a meeting, you write, "I wish I had listened more. Next time, I'll pause before responding. This humbling moment helps me understand when someone else feels embarrassed."

- **Mindfulness Pause for Self-Criticism**

Explanation of method: When you catch yourself thinking "I always mess up," pause and reframe. Say aloud or internally, "That was one moment. I'm more than my mistakes." Repeat as needed.

Example: During a drive when negative thoughts creep in, you quietly say, "I have made mistakes, but I'm loved anyway. I can choose differently next time."

The choice to accept yourself is ongoing. Sometimes grace flows easily; other days, it feels like you're fighting through thorns. Yet the steady practice of releasing harsh judgment opens the door to healing. As those judgments soften, the next natural step is learning both to give and receive forgiveness—a process that builds on self-acceptance and leads to even deeper freedom.

Forgiveness as the Doorway to New Life

You can't rewrite your story or step into freedom without forgiveness. It's the secret ingredient, and missing it leaves your life heavy and tied to old mistakes, even after you believe God's promises about your worth. Forgiveness changes everything, but it isn't a one-time event where you suddenly forget the hurt or wave away real pain. It's about letting God's mercy move through you, breaking the cycles of shame and keeping bitterness from taking root. This isn't pretending nothing happened. It's facing the wrong, yours and others', and choosing a different response: God's way, not your own. That's where real transformation starts.

Forgiveness, as Jesus modeled, is radical. Picture Joseph, sold into slavery by his own brothers. He had every reason to let anger eat away at him, to keep score, or demand payback when power shifted to his side. Instead, he forgave, not because his brothers deserved it, but because God had changed him. Read Genesis 50:20, and you see Joseph's perspective: "You intended to harm me, but God intended it for good." Jesus, suffering on the cross, looks at the people who condemned and tortured him and says, "Father, forgive them; for they know not what they do" (Luke 23:34). These moments make it clear: forgiveness for a believer is not negotiable. Colossians 3:13 spells it out: "Forgive as the Lord forgave you." That means no keeping lists, or closing your heart until others beg enough, or only forgiving when you feel like it.

You see this play out everywhere you look. Think of someone who refuses to let go of a friend's betrayal. Years pass, and they rehearse what happened, fueling every interaction with suspicion. Walls go up. Trust shrivels. Even moments of happiness get clouded by the old wound. The bitterness feels safer than the risk of being hurt again. But it poisons not just relationships, but your energy, your sleep, the way you experience joy. Real forgiveness is freedom. It is a breath of fresh air after months in a stuffy room. It invites God's love to pour in, allowing you to love others, to mend broken family ties, and to move forward without old burdens weighing you down. Healing comes as God replaces the urge for revenge with compassion. You laugh more easily, love with fewer conditions, and wake up light again.

Bitterness keeps you stuck in painful memories. It shows up as quick irritation with new friends, harsh sarcasm to loved ones, or a constant urge to relive old fights in your head. Your energy drains. Creativity and hope shrink. You find yourself comparing, grumbling, and waiting to be disappointed. You feel defensive even when nothing is wrong. Signs of this might be obsessive negative thoughts, a knot in your stomach at the mention of someone's name, or even envy toward those who seem at peace. One simple way to start breaking bitterness's grip is to make a list of memories that trigger you, then pray over each one, asking God to show you any resentment hidden there. Begin to speak forgiveness over the names and moments on that list, either quietly or out loud.

Forgiving yourself can be the hardest part. It is tempting to keep punishing yourself for old decisions, thinking you don't deserve a second chance until you've done enough good to make up for the past. But God's forgiveness is complete. He isn't asking you to earn it. He gives it freely. Start by naming the mistake honestly. Maybe you yelled at your child, or betrayed a partner's trust, or made a costly error at work. Write it down. Admit the guilt.

Say aloud: "I made a mistake, but I accept God's forgiveness and choose to forgive myself too."

In prayer or journaling, speak words of mercy to yourself the way you would encourage a friend. Instead of endless self-criticism, try saying, "That was wrong, but it does not define me. God's grace covers even this." Confession breaks the silence. Prayer invites God's viewpoint. With practice, self-forgiveness unfolds, first with small moments, then with the deeper wounds.

Try this release exercise. Picture the pain or resentment like a heavy stone you hold in your hands. Take three slow, deep breaths, feeling its weight and how it's affected your life, your thoughts, your mood, your body. Silently or in prayer, say: "I'm ready to set this down. I want freedom, real freedom." Imagine placing that stone on the ground and letting it roll away, or turning it into something light, like a feather. Ask God's peace to fill the empty space in your hands and your heart. End by saying, "Thank you for helping me let go," or writing a short note of gratitude. For example, someone struggling with anger toward an old friend might picture the anger as a burning coal, then watch it cool, turn to ash, and blow away—leaving only warmth and room for peace.

Revisit this practice whenever old wounds surface. Each time, you move closer to real freedom, making space for the deeper truth: your worth doesn't depend on your scars. As new doors open—affirming your value, breaking free from comparison—the journey goes forward. But it always starts here.

Discovering Worth: No Longer Defined by Brokenness

One life-giving habit you can begin right now is speaking affirmations about your identity in Christ aloud each morning. This might sound a little strange at first, but there's a real reason behind it. When you declare the truth out loud, you engage both your mind and body. This simple action interrupts old habits of negative self-talk and starts to rewire your mind. The more you rehearse truth, the more naturally it replaces old beliefs shaped by shame or failure.

Picture starting your day by saying, "I am God's beloved." That doesn't mean you're perfect or always have it together, but it means God's love for you is unwavering. Or, "My past does not define me; I am made new in Christ." This statement is a direct answer to guilt and regret, anchoring your worth in something bigger than your own track record. Another powerful statement: "I am forgiven." These aren't empty words; they're rooted in what scripture says about you, and each one is like planting a flag in the ground of your true identity.

Getting Practical: Building a Morning Routine

Try choosing three to five affirmations that feel meaningful to you. Here's a way to embed them right into your day:

- Write your affirmations on sticky notes or type them into your phone. Place them somewhere you'll look every single day, maybe your bathroom mirror, your car dashboard, or as your phone lock screen.

- Dedicate just a minute or two each morning to stand (or sit), say each statement aloud slowly, and pause after each one. Let the words settle in. Picture yourself living as if each affirmation were already true.

- When old thoughts pop up—"I'm a failure," "I'll never change," or "Others are better than me"—come back to your notes. Speak your affirmations again, gently but firmly, right over that old narrative.

Imagine someone named Alex, who carried around constant feelings of failure. Every morning, Alex begins with "I am made whole in Christ; my value is secure." At first, it feels awkward, but over a few weeks, Alex notices something shifting. The voice inside starts sounding less harsh, more hopeful, even in hard moments.

Tracking Growth: Journaling Small Victories

Growth isn't always dramatic. Sometimes, real progress is simply not criticizing yourself for one day, or showing kindness to someone who hurt you. You may only notice how things have changed when you pause to look back. A daily journaling practice can help you see and celebrate the steps you're taking.

- Every night, jot down one thing that reflects your new identity or a sign of healing. Did you use an affirmation to push back against self-doubt? Did you forgive yourself or someone else? Did you simply notice a blessing you once would have ignored?

- At the end of each week, review what you wrote. Look for patterns; maybe you're responding more gently to yourself, or you're comparing less often.

- Celebrate in a small, meaningful way. Maybe call a friend and tell them about your progress, whisper a prayer of gratitude, or treat yourself to a favorite coffee. These moments of celebration reinforce new habits.

Someone named Jamie once felt discouraged by slow progress. Yet, by tracking these small wins, Jamie started to see that each missed day of self-criticism, or every time they forgave a minor slight, became a little milestone, turning frustration into motivation.

Naming Your Blessings: A Gratitude Practice

Focusing on what's going well and recognizing your strengths builds lasting joy. Each week, list three God-given strengths or positive traits. Maybe you're patient, creative, or a loyal friend. Keep this running list in your journal and look over it regularly.

Once a week, try sharing one of your strengths with a friend, whether through encouragement or by offering help. Tag your gratitude by thanking God for these gifts.

For example, if you find "I am compassionate," "I am creative," and "I am persistent" on your list, thank God for each. Maybe you send a thoughtful note to someone who's having a hard time or help a friend tackle a big project.

Escaping the Trap of Comparison

Everyone gets caught up comparing themselves to others, especially after scrolling through perfectly curated moments online. This comparison can rob your sense of peace. When you notice you're comparing:

- Pause and name one unique thing about your journey or calling.

- Replace the thought with, "My path is designed for me; I am growing at my own pace."

- If comparison lingers, go back to your affirmation or gratitude list.

Each of these simple, concrete steps helps root your sense of worth in Christ rather than your history or others' approval. With practice, your inner dialogue can shift from critical to compassionate, anchoring you in the steady truth of who you are.

Summary and Reflections

Now that we've explored how embracing your story with grace, practicing forgiveness, and grounding your worth in Christ can transform your life, it's time to put these truths into action. Choose to see your past not as a chain but as a stepping stone toward freedom. Let go of bitterness and self-judgment by forgiving yourself and others, and start speaking words of healing over your heart each day. As you do, you'll find your identity shifting from brokenness to belonging, and your confidence growing stronger than ever before. This journey won't always be easy, but with each step rooted in faith and kindness, you'll move closer to the peace and joy that come from truly knowing your worth.

Where You Make Peace With Your Story

- What part of your story do you still replay with shame, and how has it shaped the way you see yourself today?

- In what ways have you been tying your identity to past mistakes instead of to who you are now?

- If you spoke to your younger self with honesty and kindness, what would you want them to hear most?

- Where are you holding onto bitterness—toward someone else or yourself—and what has it been costing you emotionally or spiritually?

- What feels hardest about forgiveness for you: letting go of the hurt, trusting God with justice, or believing you deserve grace too?

- When you compare yourself to others, what truth about your own journey do you tend to forget?

- If you truly believed that your worth is secure in Christ, how might your thoughts, choices, or relationships begin to change?

Chapter Twelve
From Chains to Champions:
Rewriting the Future

Maria found herself stuck in the same cycle every evening. No matter how hard she told herself she wouldn't reach for snacks when stress hit, her hand would betray her before she even realized it. She knew she wanted to change, wanted to feel freer, lighter, but old habits kept pulling her back like invisible chains. It wasn't just the snacking; it was the pattern of giving up on herself whenever things got tough. Deep down, she wondered if real change was even possible or if this was just how life had to be. Many of us recognize that feeling: trying to break free but somehow ending up right where we started. What keeps us caught in these loops, and is there a way to truly move beyond them?

Creating Your Blueprint for Personal Change

Choosing to change begins with looking inward. People often find themselves repeating familiar patterns, reacting the same way to stress, falling into old routines, or circling back to self-limiting habits. The desire to grow meets a wall when these cycles remain unseen. Facing discomfort and taking full stock of your current routines clears a path toward real freedom. Avoiding difficult truths actually gives them more control, but recognition brings the power to choose a new response next time. Patterns become possibilities only when you see them for what they are.

Slip-ups often come from places that feel impossible to change. Many adults get stuck repeating decisions, conversations, or reactions that don't match the life they want. Without a clear sense of what triggers setbacks, whether it's stress, boredom, fear, or fatigue, it is easy to stumble. By zooming in on behaviors and emotions around difficult moments, hidden strengths and roadblocks show themselves.

Self-Inventory Exercise

- Identify three areas in your life where challenges and frustrations return again and again, such as late-night snacking, heated arguments with a partner, or losing motivation at work.

- For each area, pay attention to what happens just before you lose your footing. Is it a specific thought, a negative emotion, or a certain situation? Write it down. For example: "Before I argue with my partner, I feel unappreciated." "Right before I procrastinate, I think, 'This will never get done anyway.'"

- Next to each area, write one strength or trait that you often call on, even in small ways. Maybe you have patience, a knack for seeing humor, or a deep sense of loyalty.

- Beside every strength, add one vulnerability or tendency that throws a wrench in your plans, such as distraction, defensiveness, or indecision. Then, match it with one small, practical action or source of support. If self-doubt trips you up, could a sticky note with encouragement on your bathroom mirror help? If you get distracted, could turning off smartphone notifications make things easier? Small moves plant the seeds for big change.

Reflecting with courage turns discomfort into discovery. Someone who overspends when anxious learns to spot this urge, recognizes their natural creativity with budgets, and asks a trusted friend to check in each Friday before the weekend shopping trips.

Vision: Crafting Your Future Self

Visualizing what's possible creates an engine for hope. When you picture your best self, imagination shifts energy away from what's wrong and into what could be. Committing these aspirations to writing transforms daydreams into promises. Allow yourself to dream boldly. Think about who you want to be and what changes would bring ease, confidence, and meaning.

Future Self Letter Exercise

- Block off ten minutes for quiet, uninterrupted writing.

- Address a letter from the person you hope to be one year from today, writing to your present self.

- Spell out three visible changes in your daily routine, behaviors, or choices, such as walking for thirty minutes after dinner, starting each morning with five deep breaths, or choosing one family night per week with no screens.

- Share one emotional or spiritual quality you wish to embody more fully, such as steady optimism, calm, or clear boundaries.

- Finish your letter with a personal promise for tough days, like: "No matter how many times I slip, I will keep moving toward my goals."

Taking time to write grounds visions in reality. Someone hoping to end comfort-eating imagines their future self enjoying food mindfully, savoring dinners with friends, and embracing a new sense of self-respect.

Goal Setting: Simple Steps Matter

Real progress grows from realistic, meaningful goals, not just big leaps. Often, small wins outshine grand ambitions by building confidence steadily. Choosing goals that reflect your deepest values holds you steady when motivation dips. Values shaped by faith, kindness, or service can point you to what truly matters, filtering out distractions.

Goal Setting Exercise

- Choose one focus area from your self-inventory, the place where you're most ready to grow.

- Write a goal for the next thirty days that is clear, measurable, and aligned with your beliefs. For example: "I will pause for a moment of gratitude every morning before looking at my phone."

- Break this primary goal into weekly milestones that feel doable, such as "This week, I will keep a gratitude journal for three days."

- Note how following through will honor your core values or faith. For instance: "I want my daily actions to reflect thankfulness and trust."

A reader trying to curb impulsive spending might set a one-month goal to track every purchase, breaking it down to one week at a time, rooted in the value of stewardship.

Building Accountability

Lasting change depends on support, not willpower alone. When resilience dips, accountability keeps goals in sight. Choose someone who offers both honesty and encouragement, a friend, a mentor, or a support group member.

Accountability Check-In Exercise

- Pick a person with integrity who understands your journey and will hold you to your word.

- Ask them to meet weekly or every other week, face-to-face or virtually.

- Create three check-in questions you will both use at each meeting: "What progress did I see this week?" "Where did I struggle?" "What is my next micro-step?"

- If a check-in falls through, set an immediate backup plan, like a ten-minute phone call or sending a text summary.

The blueprint you create now sets a ripple in motion. Later, you'll discover how this personal shift radiates out, touching others and expanding hope far beyond your own story.

The Ripple Effect: Impacting Others and Leaving a Legacy

Self-awareness makes hidden habits and patterns visible. With that knowledge, people begin to create a clear vision for themselves and set new goals that reflect who they want to be. When someone decides to break a cycle of self-doubt, their world not only changes for themselves, but their new direction influences everyone around them. The quiet courage to pause, reflect, and choose a different response can spark curiosity in siblings, friends, and peers who witness the difference. People start to notice when someone they love becomes less reactive, more supportive, and openly hopeful about the future. Simple acts like pausing to breathe during frustration or choosing a kind word over sarcasm often invite questions or even admiration.

Picture a young woman who grew up in a family where criticism came faster than praise. She begins the work of changing her self-talk, setting boundaries, and seeking support. As she becomes more confident, her brother starts to notice she is no longer retreating or snapping back during arguments. He feels safer, more valued, and over time finds himself ready to speak his own truth. Friends begin asking her for advice about handling difficult conversations because they see her radiating more calm and possibility than ever before. Her personal growth gives others permission to imagine themselves changing, too.

Ripples Through Family and Peers

When someone breaks free from negative patterns, the impact does not go unnoticed. Imagine a father who grew up with yelling as the only form of discipline. Determined to do better, he works through his anger triggers, chooses soft words, and apologizes when he falls short. His children grow up learning that mistakes are not shameful. These kids carry more confidence to school, make friends easily, and are less likely to carry those old patterns forward. Other parents see his approach and ask what changed. Soon, neighborhood playdates become less tense.

The spread of healthy habits is not dramatic at first. Many times, it is the hopeful shift in a single family member's attitude that signals something is different. An aunt who learns to listen and encourage leads her nieces and nephews to confide in her, rather than hide. A friend who practices gratitude starts group chats where everyone shares what went well that week. Positivity catches on, often spreading quietly but deeply. These are not grand gestures; they are everyday choices, putting down the phone during dinner, listening before judging, or saying sorry with sincerity. All these actions combine to rewrite what is possible for everyone connected.

Shaping a New Legacy for Future Generations

The biggest changes often reveal themselves across generations. When someone sets aside old coping skills and learns to respond with patience, their children experience family life as a haven rather than a battleground. Small rituals start to form: a mother and her son share a nightly gratitude practice; a father chooses affirming words before school instead of warnings. These rituals become new family traditions. Children in these homes are more willing to talk about problems, less likely to feel ashamed of their feelings, and better equipped to form healthy relationships. As these children grow, they instinctively offer the same warmth and openness to their partners and, one day, their own kids. The generational story shifts from frustration and fear to acceptance and hope.

Take the example of a couple who decide to break the silence around mental health in their home. They discuss emotions at the dinner table and show that it is safe to admit when they are overwhelmed. Their children learn how to name feelings and ask for help. Over time, relatives notice less conflict and more laughter at family gatherings. By making change visible and consistent, one family creates a ripple that stretches far beyond their own four walls.

Transforming Workplaces and Community Spaces

Change in the personal sphere soon reaches the professional world. In a small business, a manager who once avoided feedback now models accountability. She welcomes input from her team, owns her mistakes, and sets clear expectations. The team feels respected, and conflict drops. Inspired by her example, another team leader tries weekly check-ins and sees trust grow. The workplace shifts from suspicion and blame to collaboration and innovation. In these environments, motivation runs high, and people take pride in what they do because they feel seen and heard.

A warehouse team once struggled with low morale and constant turnover. After one employee began sharing strategies for stress management and better communication, small changes took root. Lunch breaks became a time for sharing wins instead of complaints. Over months, productivity improved, sick days declined, and new hires stayed longer. One person's commitment to growth changed the story for an entire workplace.

The journey of transformation gathers energy from small, daily practices. Simple tools like speaking affirmations, taking a moment to reflect on a challenge, or writing down three things to be thankful for keep the momentum going. Surrendering perfection or grudges makes room for healthier habits. These everyday steps help anchor change both for the individual and for everyone in their circle.

A Daily Recipe for Sustaining Freedom and Joy

The first words and thoughts that fill your morning are like the building blocks that shape your expectations and mood for the whole day. If you start with doubt or distraction, you're already trying to run uphill. That's why a Morning Declaration, speaking your identity and intent out loud, helps you claim your ground before anything else can. It's about choosing to rewrite old labels with new, faith-filled truth. You model bold change, first for yourself, then for anyone who sees how you carry yourself into your daily life.

To create your own Morning Declaration, stand or sit where you usually wake up, feet grounded, eyes open or closed. Breathe slowly. Speak words of purpose and belonging. You don't need to sound polished. You just need to be honest and present. Try at least one of the following daily, adapting as you discover what rings true:

- "I am a child of God, deeply loved and made for today's purpose."

- "I choose to let hope define my steps and kindness guard my words."

- "God, I trust You to walk with me through whatever I face today."

The more you declare these truths, the more your mind expects good things—confidence grows quietly, reshaping old pathways. If it feels awkward at first, stick with it; new growth needs steady watering, not perfection.

Settling your mind with scripture before you tackle the urgent or noisy parts of the day gives you a new inner compass. Bible Meditation isn't just reading words, it's letting them interrupt your rush, planting calm and focus. This helps you not just react from old habits, but respond with purpose, like someone who knows their story is changing in real time. Here's how to practice:

1. Select a short scripture or passage, maybe one that addresses a challenge or longing you feel today. If lost, start with the Psalms—Psalm 23:1, for example.

2. Read the verse slowly. Notice which words stand out or stir something in you.

3. Spend two or three minutes reflecting on how it connects to your current journey. Picture the phrase, repeat it, or whisper it under your breath.

4. Ask what this verse might invite you to do or believe today.

5. Jot a brief insight, a question, or a prayer in a notebook or your phone.For instance, reading "The Lord is my shepherd; I lack nothing," you might write: "Today, I choose to trust I will have what I need, even when I can't see what's ahead." The act of writing grounds your reflection and keeps the wisdom close, especially when challenges show up later.

Simple moments of joy are everywhere, but sometimes you need to practice noticing them before they leave their trace on your heart. Joy Journaling carves out space each day to capture gratitude. This strengthens your resilience and invites hope to grow roots. When you begin, grab a small notebook, the notes app on your phone, or even the back of an envelope.

Write down three things you're thankful for each day, no matter how ordinary. Prompts might help: What made you smile today? Who offered you kindness or patience? What simple pleasure gave you a spark—sun streaming through the window, your first sip of coffee, a passing laugh with a co-worker? For example, an entry might be: "Grateful for my morning walk, the friendly nod from the neighbor, the cozy socks I found at the bottom of the drawer."

At the end of each week, page through your entries. Notice the patterns; are certain names, places, or changes appearing? Maybe you'll see how your heart's shifting, or spot strengths and themes, like courage or faithfulness, that weren't obvious before. Joy accumulates, and as it does, your story reads brighter to you and those around you.

Letting go at day's end is its own kind of freedom. When life's worries, guilt, or unfinished to-dos cling tight, Evening Surrender creates room for rest and renewal. Here's how to practice: Before bed, pause and remember your day. Name anything heavy like regrets, anxieties, disappointments, with honesty. In your own words or in silence, offer each up to God. Imagine setting them down beside your bed, removed from your chest. Pray or speak a gentle permission to yourself, such as: "God, I give you what I can't carry tonight. Thank you for loving me as I am. Help me rest and wake ready." Repeat this habit, trusting that each surrender isn't weakness, but strength gained back for tomorrow.

Woven together, these small deliberate choices, if spoken with truth, meditation, gratitude, and surrender, will build real momentum. Your journey ripples out, not by dramatic leaps, but through these quiet, daily acts that rewrite what freedom and hope look like, for you and for those who follow your example.

Bringing It All Together

Now that you have the tools to create your personal blueprint for change, it's time to take those first brave steps toward a better you. By understanding your patterns, setting clear goals, and practicing daily habits like gratitude and reflection, you're not just transforming your own life; you're lighting the way for others around you. Each small choice you make builds momentum, shaping a future filled with freedom, joy, and hope. Keep moving forward with courage and kindness, knowing that your growth creates ripples far beyond what you can see today.

What You Must Ask Yourself to Break the Cycle

- Where do you notice yourself falling into the same patterns, even when you genuinely want change?

- What usually happens right before you slip back into an old habit—what thought, feeling, or situation shows up first?

- Which strength do you already have that could support your growth if you used it more intentionally?

- What fear or belief has been quietly convincing you that real change might not last for you?

- When you picture your future self one year from now, what daily habit or choice feels most important to start practicing today?

- Who could help keep you accountable without shaming you—and what would it look like to ask for that support?

- If your personal growth created a ripple effect, how might it change the way your family, friends, or community experience you?

Conclusion

You've made it to this final page, but in many ways, this isn't an ending at all; it's a powerful new beginning. When you started this book, you probably had a simple question: Am I holding myself back? Maybe the doubts crept in quietly, or maybe the evidence was loud and clear, a pattern of unfinished goals, strained relationships, or spiritual struggles that couldn't be solved by sheer willpower alone. The heart of this entire journey has been about debunking the myth that self-sabotage is just a character flaw or weakness. Instead, it's often a tangled mix of learned behaviors, unconscious fears, and distorted beliefs, shaped by both internal stories and external influences, and, yes, even our faith journeys. My mission from the very first chapter was to shine a gentle yet honest light on those hidden corners, not just so you could spot the traps, but so you'd be fully equipped to rise above them.

If you pause for a moment and look back, you'll notice you're leaving behind more than just unhealthy habits. You're stepping out of old cycles, equipped now with practical strategies and spiritual tools that are designed to go the distance. There's a transformation already underway within you, a shift from reacting automatically to your own self-sabotage, to responding intentionally, fueled by both personal insight and authentic faith. Where once you might have felt powerless or stuck, now you can see clear options, rooted in new ways of thinking and grounded in your relationship with God. You aren't just moving forward; you're being empowered to live differently.

Let's bring together the threads of everything you've learned, because sometimes perspective is clearest once you step back and see the whole tapestry. Early in this book, we looked honestly at what self-sabotage really means. It's easy to underestimate how deep its roots can run, showing up not just in dramatic failures, but in everyday choices—the "small" procrastinations, the critical inner dialogue, the quiet moments where we doubt our own worth or capacity to change. We learned how these patterns don't come from nowhere; they often begin as survival mechanisms, shaped by early experiences, cultural messages, and, yes, even church teachings that unintentionally plant seeds of shame or limitation.

From there, we drew from psychological research to understand why our brains latch onto familiar—even harmful—habits. We talked about triggers, defense mechanisms, and the science behind motivation and habit formation. But we didn't stop with the psychology textbook. We went deeper into the way your spiritual life intersects with your mental health. For too long, conversations about Christian faith and emotional well-being have happened in separate rooms. This book invites you to break down that wall, to see how biblical wisdom and modern psychology go hand-in-hand, both pointing toward healing and wholeness instead of hiding or guilt.

We opened the pages of scripture to find examples of real people who wrestled with their own self-defeating cycles—think of Moses' doubts, Peter's denials, or Elijah's despair. These weren't perfect heroes but relatable individuals whose struggles were met with grace, patience, and transformational encounters with God. Their stories remind us that self-sabotage isn't something to be ashamed of. It's part of the shared human story, but it doesn't have to be the last word. Time and again, we saw how God's response isn't condemnation, but an invitation, a call to step into a fuller life, with support, guidance, and unconditional love as the foundation.

In exploring the relational impact of self-sabotage, we got honest about the consequences. How many friendships falter or marriages strain because we push others away before they can reject us? How often do we choose isolation over vulnerability, comfort over growth? But we also discovered the power of community, accountability, and healthy boundaries—not as obligations, but as sources of renewal. Just as faith is lived out in relationship, breaking free from self-sabotage is something we do alongside others. The path to healing is rarely solitary, and letting trusted people in is one of the most courageous acts you can take.

Change wouldn't mean much without action steps, so throughout this book, you worked through practical breakthrough strategies. From recognizing your triggers to rewriting negative thought scripts, from practicing self-compassion to embracing daily spiritual disciplines, you learned that freedom doesn't come from a single "aha!" moment. It comes from thousands of small, consistent choices. Spiritual tools—like prayer, meditation on scripture, worship, and seeking wise counsel—aren't just religious checkboxes. They are lifelines, connecting you to God's strength when your own runs short. At the same time, the practical exercises drawn from behavioral science give you frameworks for real change—ways to gradually shift your thoughts, reactions, and habits through intentional practice.

One of the most important messages you absorbed along the way is this: your identity matters. Self-sabotage thrives in the shadows of confusion about who we are. When your sense of self is anchored in old failures or labels, it's easy to fall into the same destructive loops. This book challenged you to reimagine your identity, not as someone doomed to repeat the past, but as a person made in the image of a loving and redemptive God—someone uniquely gifted, called, and capable of change. As you embraced this truth, you began to see setbacks as opportunities for growth, not as confirmation of defeat. Your past may shape you, but it doesn't define you. With each page, you crafted a new mental map, one that routes around the old roadblocks and leads toward an identity rooted in both faith and resilience.

So, what does all of this mean for your life going forward? It's tempting to close a book like this and immediately worry about slipping back into what's familiar. That's normal. The lie of self-sabotage is that it tells you nothing ever really changes. But you've already proven otherwise, simply by engaging with these ideas and imagining what a different future might look like. The tools you now hold aren't magic wands; they require time, reinforcement, and grace for yourself on the hard days. But they are powerful, especially when used consistently. Remember, the aim isn't perfection; it's progress. Each moment you catch yourself before repeating an old habit, every time you reach out for help instead of isolating, and any step you take toward honesty and openness, these are victories.

More importantly, you no longer have to fight this battle alone. Faith offers you a steady anchor, something unchanging to hold onto as you navigate the ups and downs. God's perspective of you hasn't wavered. You are loved, forgiven, and called to growth, and as you lean into His presence, the lie of hopelessness starts to lose its grip. If you forget everything else, remember that redemption is always possible, no matter how many times you've circled the same mountain. Change, lasting and genuine, is not out of reach. It's within you and around you, sparked by courage, kindled by faith, and sustained by hope.

As you turn the last page, take a breath. Reflect on the journey you've taken inside these chapters. Let the lessons settle in, but don't let them stay stuck as theory. Step forward. Try. Risk failing. Trust that each effort matters. And above all, know that the process of overcoming self-sabotage is lifelong, but so is the potential for transformation. You are now equipped, empowered, and encouraged to choose a new direction, again and again, grounded in truth, strengthened by faith, and inspired by possibility.

The next chapter belongs to you.